NEWFOUNDLAND

SOUTH
AFRICA

AUSTRALIA

NEW ZEALAND

FRANCE

MOROCCO

GERMANY

FINLAND

PORTUGAL

BELGIUM

NORWAY

TURKEY

EGYPT

HOLY LAND

SPAIN

HOLLAND

ITALY

SWITZERLAND

THE "PEEPS" SERIES

PEEPS AT MANY LANDS AND CITIES

AUSTRALIA	FRANCE	NEWFOUNDLAND
BELGIUM	GERMANY	NEW YORK
BERLIN	GREECE	NEW ZEALAND
BURMA	HOLLAND	NORWAY
CANADA	HOLY LAND	PARIS
CEYLON	HUNGARY	PORTUGAL
*CHINA	ICELAND	ROME
CORSICA	*INDIA	*RUSSIA
DELHI AND THE	IRELAND	*SCOTLAND
DURBAR	ITALY	*SIAM
DENMARK	JAMAICA	SOUTH AFRICA
EDINBURGH	*JAPAN	SOUTH SEAS
*EGYPT	JAVA	SPAIN
EGYPT, ANCIENT	KASHMIR	SWEDEN
ENGLAND	KOREA	SWITZERLAND
FINLAND	LONDON	TURKEY
FLORENCE	*MOROCCO	WALES

* Also to be had in French

PEEPS AT NATURE

WILD FLOWERS AND THEIR WONDERFUL WAYS	BIRD LIFE OF THE SEASONS
BRITISH FERNS, CLUB-MOSSES AND HORSETAILS	BRITISH BUTTERFLIES
BRITISH LAND MAMMALS	NATURAL HISTORY OF THE GARDEN
	ROMANCE OF THE ROCKS

PEEPS AT THE HEAVENS

PEEPS AT HERALDRY

HOMES OF MANY LANDS—INDIA

PEEPS AT HISTORY

AMERICA (U.S.A.)	INDIA
THE BARBARY ROVERS	JAPAN
CANADA	SCOTLAND
HOLLAND	

PEEPS AT GREAT RAILWAYS

THE GREAT WESTERN RAILWAY
THE LONDON AND NORTH-WESTERN RAILWAY
THE NORTH-EASTERN AND GREAT NORTHERN RAILWAYS
THE SOUTH-EASTERN AND CHATHAM AND LONDON, BRIGHTON AND SOUTH COAST RAILWAYS

PEEPS AT INDUSTRIES

(With Illustrations in black and white only)

RUBBER	SUGAR	TEA

PUBLISHED BY A. AND C. BLACK, 4, 5 AND 6 SOHO SQUARE, LONDON, W.

AGENTS

AMERICA	THE MACMILLAN COMPANY
	64 & 66 FIFTH AVENUE, NEW YORK
AUSTRALASIA . . .	OXFORD UNIVERSITY PRESS
	205 FLINDERS LANE, MELBOURNE
CANADA	THE MACMILLAN COMPANY OF CANADA, LTD.
	ST. MARTIN'S HOUSE, 70 BOND STREET, TORONTO
INDIA	MACMILLAN & COMPANY, LTD.
	MACMILLAN BUILDING, BOMBAY
	309 BOW BAZAAR STREET, CALCUTTA

COLUMN OF MARCUS AURELIUS, BUILT
IN THE SECOND CENTURY

PEEPS AT GREAT CITIES

ROME

BY

C. T. GENN

WITH TWELVE FULL-PAGE ILLUSTRATIONS
IN COLOUR

LONDON
ADAM AND CHARLES BLACK
1911

CONTENTS

LIST OF ILLUSTRATIONS

ROME

CHAPTER I

A FIRST IMPRESSION

ROME, which has been called "Immortal Rome," and " Rome the Eternal," stands alone in the world, not only on account of the beauty and interest of her monuments and the wonderful romance of her history, but because the story conveyed by those monuments, and the long continuance of that history, afford us such a link between past and present as we possess in no other way. Hundreds of years before we have any record of the early inhabitants of our own island, Rome existed on the Palatine Hill, and on the Palatine Hill to-day may be seen the massive and still imposing remains of buildings whose stones were laid more than two thousand years ago.

With such thoughts as these in our minds, it is surprising and a little bewildering, on a first arrival in Rome, to find ourselves, on leaving the bustle of the station, plunged into the busy streets of

Rome

an apparently quite modern city. Electric trams glide past in all directions, taxi-cabs, tradesmen's carts, and motors crowd the streets, which in this quarter are wide and well paved, and altogether there is little to remind us that we are in a city whose history extends over more than twenty centuries.

But this feeling of disenchantment soon wears off as we leave the modern part of the town and begin to explore the older quarters. Here many delightful surprises await us. The streets, it is true, are narrow and dirty, quite particularly muddy in wet weather and remarkably dusty when it is dry and fine, but always full of interest. The remains of old temples—in some cases now used as dwelling-places—ancient churches, historic palaces, and fragments of once splendid arches and gateways, are to be found crowded in between the high, shabby, but picturesque old tenement-houses now occupied by the poorer inhabitants, as well as in the more prosperous streets, which still retain much of their ancient dignity.

The principal street in Rome is called the Corso (race-course), from the fact that it was formerly used for races of riderless horses, a sport of which the Romans were passionately fond. It was well adapted for such a purpose, being nearly a mile long and perfectly straight.

6

A First Impression

This long, narrow, and, at first sight, rather shabby-looking street contains so much of historic interest that volumes might be written about it without exhausting the subject. Many a house, now let off in flats, with the ground-floor used as a shop, has an eventful and romantic history, having been the palace of some great Roman family, and, perhaps, in bygone days the scene of stirring events or even of terrible tragedies. It has been said that the very stones of Rome cry blood, and, indeed, if stones could speak, some of these ancient houses could reveal innumerable tales of violence and treachery, and also many a story of devoted courage and heroism.

But the Corso, as we see it now, on a fine afternoon, is far from suggesting gloomy or even serious ideas. At such a time it presents a lively and animated scene, for all Rome seems to turn out. Everybody is either going to, or returning from, the Pincian Gardens: the most popular resort for afternoon drives and walks, especially on Sundays and Thursdays, when there is an excellent band to add to the other attractions of this beautiful park. The pavement in some parts of the Corso is very narrow, being hardly more than three feet in width; the roadway during the fashionable hours for driving is almost blocked with carriages, so that it becomes really difficult to make one's way through the over-

Rome

crowded street, and a stranger not unnaturally
wonders why the inhabitants of a great city should
put up with such a state of things. But the Romans
have always loved a crowd, and the jostle and con-
fusion seem if anything to add to their pleasure.
They form into groups and stand laughing and
talking on the narrow pavement, regardless of the
crowd surging around them and of the unlucky
wayfarers who may wish to pass and are constantly
obliged to step out into the road, braving the traffic
as best they may. It is true that the Romans themselves never seem to be in a hurry, and it is a very
rare thing to see one of them walking quickly along
the street as if he really wanted to reach any
particular place at any particular time. The very
fire-engines seem to a stranger to move at a leisurely
pace. The only things which go quickly in Rome
are the rickety open cabs, drawn by wiry, spirited
little horses which, urged on by their drivers, dash
round sharp corners and plunge along the crowded
streets at a break-neck speed, except, indeed, when
they are hired by the hour, in which case their pace
at once becomes sedate and even funereal.

THE "SPANISH STEPS" LEADING UP TO THE
PINCIAN HILL. *Page 10*

CHAPTER II

SOME EVERYDAY SCENES IN ROME

A SPECIAL charm of the Roman streets consists in the variety of colour and form in the costumes to be seen, though, strange to say, the women do not as a rule contribute much to the brightness of the general effect, for it is very rare to see a fashionably dressed Italian lady walking out of doors in Rome, while the women of the middle and lower classes show a strong preference for black. It is therefore to the men that we are indebted for most of the picturesque and graceful garments we see in the streets.

There are in Rome a large number of seminaries and colleges where young men are trained for the priesthood, and each seminary has its own special costume, consisting in most cases of a long dark cassock, with a sash and other decorations of some vivid colour. The dress worn by the students of the German seminary is, however, much more beautiful and striking than any of the others, being red of a very rich shade, and the effect is most picturesque when the young men are seen passing in large companies through the narrow streets, across the public squares, or up the steps of some

Rome

grey old church. The Romans are rather fond of giving nicknames, and speak familiarly of these gorgeously clad youths as the *gamberi cotti*, or "boiled lobsters."

Besides the students, there are the different orders of monks, in their long flowing habits and cowls of various tints, of which the most beautiful is certainly the soft creamy white worn by the Dominicans. Then the artists' models—of whom there are a great many in Rome—are often to be seen in their quaint costumes of bright and varied colours; those who are disengaged lying half-asleep, or chatting merrily, on any convenient flight of steps, or even squatting on the pavements in the artists' quarter, wherever they can find a welcome patch of sunlight, while the more fortunate ones, who are employed in some studio, are usually to be met between twelve and one o'clock, which is their luncheon-hour, in the neighbourhood of the Spanish Steps: a beautiful, broad, and very high flight of steps leading from the Spanish Square up on to the Pincian Hill. At the foot of the steps are rows of flower-stalls, which, with their masses of brilliant blossoms, help to make this one of the most charming spots in Rome. Here the models stroll about, gossiping and eating their lunch, which often consists of a hunch of bread and a slice of sausage or some minced-up meat rolled in cabbage: a delicacy which may be bought at many of the humble eating-houses for two or three half-pence.

Some of the models are quite young children, and even babies in arms are made use of in this way. Small boys in green breeches, yellow waistcoats, and red jackets, or some such motley costume, seem to find their chief pleasure in freedom of movement after long and tedious posing, and never apparently tire of running up the steps and sliding down the broad stone balustrade ; but even the very little ones have an eye to business, for no sooner do they see a stranger with a camera in search of a suitable subject for a snapshot than they run up eagerly, offering to pose, arranging themselves in what they consider striking attitudes in the hope of receiving a small tip for their services.

There are many delightful ways of spending a penny in the streets of Rome. If you happen to be hungry, you may for this sum buy a large slab of very satisfying cake or pudding ; if it is hot weather, you may have an ice with a glass of coloured syrup and water ; or, if you prefer it, you may buy a goodly supply of a sort of cream toffee from the stall where it is made and sold, in which case you have the added pleasure of watching the delicious sticky compound tossed, pulled, twisted, and cut into sections before making your purchase. But, more attractive still, if you are of a sporting turn of mind, are the delights of the halfpenny roulette-table, where a very simple form of gambling may be indulged in.

The proprietor has in front of him a circular table, round which are arranged apples—partly cooked and coated with shiny caramel—figs, dates, and raisins, threaded on straws or thin bits of stick, and many other tempting morsels. In the middle of the table is a revolving button, with a pointer attached to it ; these rest on a card marked with numbers from one to ten. The proud possessor of a halfpenny, having paid his money, twists the button, when round flies the pointer, eagerly watched by the little knot of spectators, who never fail to gather round this fascinating contrivance ; if the needle as it stops points to the space marked *one*, the player may choose only one of the above-named delicacies, and is considered to have had bad luck ; but should it point to five or a higher number, he is loudly congratulated as he proceeds with great care and deliberation to select his booty. The owner of the stall reminds him jocosely that he cannot stay there all day, and also that the rule " what you touch you take " must be strictly observed, while the wistful eyes and outstretched hands of his companions eloquently invite him to share his winnings.

A delightful place in which to pass an idle hour is the market-place known to the Romans as the

Some Everyday Scenes in Rome

Campo dei Fiori ("Field of Flowers"), but familiarly called amongst the English and American visitors by the less picturesque name of Rag Fair. Wednesday being market-day, is the best time for seeing Rag Fair in its glory, but most of the business is done early in the day, as many of the stall-holders go away about one o'clock.

The wares exposed for sale are so various that it is difficult to say what may not be bought there, from an ancient gold-embroidered vestment or altar-cloth to a pair of blue spectacles or a halfpenny-worth of cooked chestnuts. There are rows of stalls for the sale of second-hand ornaments, all warranted (by the vendor) to be genuine antiques, trays of unset jewels, strings of beads, lucky charms, and odd filigree buttons. These stalls, as well as those where old brocade and lace are on sale, are always surrounded by foreigners on the look out for curios, there being a mistaken impression that it is possible to pick up wonderful bargains in Rag Fair, where the prices are actually quite as high as those asked in the more orthodox curiosity shops.

The vegetable, flower, and fruit-stalls are a pretty sight at all seasons of the year, and the part of the market where old brass and copper pots and vases are sold is very attractive. The two rows of stalls whose stock-in-trade consists of cheap articles of clothing are of little interest to visitors, but are a good deal patronized by the poor people of the city.

Besides the stall-holders, there are plenty of itinerant hawkers in the market, selling fruit, nuts, dried beans, tape, cough-lozenges, hairpins, buttons, cakes, and many other necessary articles, too numerous to mention.

Altogether Rag Fair on a Wednesday morning is an amusing and fascinating place.

CHAPTER III

HOW ROMULUS BUILT THE CITY

No one can be long in Rome without having his thoughts carried back to ancient times, and it is impossible to feel much interest in the old monuments and ruins unless we have at least some knowledge of their past history and associations.

So, when we visit the Palatine Hill, the beautiful surroundings gain an added charm from the knowledge that we are standing on the very spot where the first stones of Rome were laid.

The story of Romulus, the founder of the city, and his brother Remus, which has been handed down to us for more than 2,700 years, is that a certain wicked King Amulius of Alba, having usurped the throne of his brother Numitor, was so

How Romulus Built the City

afraid lest the son and daughter of Numitor should assert their rightful claims, that he condemned the son to die a very cruel death, and imprisoned the daughter, who was called Rhea Silvia, in a temple. Thinking he had successfully provided against all danger from the descendants of Numitor, he now hoped to enjoy fully the fruits of his wrong action n wresting the kingly power from his elder brother. You may therefore imagine his anger and dismay when he learned that Rhea Silvia was the mother of twin sons, of whom the god Mars was said to be the father. In a passion of mingled wrath and fear, he determined to destroy both mother and children, and commanded that they should be thrown into the Tiber and left to perish.

The river was at that time running so high that it had overflowed its banks, and, though the mother was drowned, the cradle containing the two babies was washed up on to the shore near the Palatine, where, as the waters subsided, it caught on some bushes, and was left with the two boys still lying safe and sound within it.

But, tiny and helpless as they were, they must even then have perished but for the timely appearance of a friendly she-wolf, who tended and suckled them. This strange foster-mother was helped in her task by a woodpecker, who daily brought the children morsels of food in her beak.

Rome

One day a shepherd, named Faustulus, found the two children, and, struck with pity for them and wonder at the miraculous way in which they had been preserved, took them home to his wife, who, though she had many boys of her own, received them kindly and cared for them, just as she did for her own family.

So it came about that Romulus and Remus spent their youth on the Palatine Hill, and when, in course of time, their royal descent was discovered, and Amulius had been punished for all his crimes by dethronement and death, their grandfather, Numitor, now restored to power, granted them a domain which included the Palatine.

On one point the two brothers were quite agreed. They both wished to build a city, but, unfortunately, they differed with regard to the site which would be best for building, Romulus being strongly in favour of the Palatine, while Remus just as strongly preferred the neighbouring hill of the Aventine. Each brother had many supporters, and when the dispute had raged for a long time it was decided that the Augurs should be consulted. The Augurs were men who claimed the power of divining the will of the gods, and foretelling future events, by observing the flight of birds and other phenomena of the same kind, and they directed that Romulus should wait on the Palatine and Remus on the

How Romulus Built the City

Aventine until some sign or omen was observed which might decide the question.

When Remus and his friends returned from their watch on the Aventine, saying they had seen six vultures, the omen was considered a very good one; but when Romulus declared that he had seen no fewer than twelve of the same birds, and was supported in his statement by all who had been with him, the dispute was decided in his favour, and he began his preparations for building on the Palatine.

This story of Romulus and Remus, although much of it must be legendary, took such firm hold on the minds and imaginations of the Roman people, that from the earliest ages the subject of the motherly she-wolf with the two babies whom she rescued, has been a first favourite with the sculptor, the painter, and the artificer.

There is a wonderful bronze wolf in the Capitol which is said to have been cast in the fifth century B.C., though the figures of the children were added much later, and this particular group is constantly reproduced and copied in all manner of ways. It is seen on the fronts of buildings, public and private, as a decoration to arches, fountains, etc., on vases and other ornaments in metal or china; you may find it painted on the plate you use at dessert, or even see it dangling as a tiny charm on a watch-chain.

Rome

The most important day in the whole year to the shepherd-colonists of the Palatine was the 21st of April, for it was the festival of Pales, the goddess of shepherds, and this was the date in the year 2754 B.C. chosen by Romulus for beginning his great undertaking.

The building of a city was not undertaken without various solemn ceremonies, by which the ground was consecrated, and the gods propitiated to insure their favour for the new town.

First of all, a hollow was dug in the centre of the piece of ground chosen for building; each of the new citizens threw into it a handful of earth brought from his native place, and offerings of the fruits of the earth were added, with prayers and invocations to the gods to look favourably on their city. The ground was then made level again; an altar was raised on which a fire was lighted; and the consecration of the central part of the city was complete.

In order to trace out and consecrate its boundaries, Romulus harnessed a bull and a cow, both snow-white and of perfect beauty, to a bronze plough, and marked out the exact line where the walls were to stand. As he ploughed he prayed aloud to the gods for the success and prosperity of his work, asking that the city they were about to build might last for many ages, and might become all-powerful.

CHAPTER IV

IMPERIAL PALACES AND THE HOUSEHOLD
OF A GREAT LADY

THE Palatine Hill, on which the first modest foundations of Rome were laid, was destined in Imperial times to be the site of those wonderful palaces whose ruins are still in sufficiently good preservation to make the Palatine one of the most interesting spots in Rome. These buildings are generally called the Palaces of the Cæsars.

In learning a little about these Imperial dwellings we shall learn something of how the great and powerful Romans lived in the days of the Empire, and be able to contrast their luxury and magnificence with the simpler life and surroundings of the ordinary citizens. For it must not be forgotten that the persons who are most prominent in history and who, during their lives, sat in the seats of the mighty, were a very small number as compared with the great bulk of the people.

While the Cæsars dwelt in Palaces—accounts of which read like fairy-tales—numberless Roman families were living contentedly in small confined houses in the narrow, crowded streets of the city, and in the classes below these respectable householders were the servants and slaves, who formed a very large proportion of the population of Rome.

Anything like a full description of the remains of the Imperial Palaces on the Palatine would fill a volume; but we may gain some idea of what they once were from accounts given at different times by writers who saw with their own eyes the glories that we can only dimly behold by the help of imagination.

One writer describes the state entrance to the Palace of Augustus, on whose chief arch the Emperor had placed a group of sculpture, representing a great chariot, driven by Apollo and Diana, and drawn by four horses, the whole group being carved out of one immense block of marble. Another mentions a colossal gate with marble pillars, each nearly thirty feet in height, and we are also told of a bronze statue of Augustus in the guise of Apollo, which was about eight times as large as life.

On passing the entrance to the Palace, a visitor found himself in the most splendid halls that have ever been formed by the hand of man—marble pavements, successions of beautiful fluted marble pillars, not white but tinged with a warm golden hue, exquisite statuary representing gods, goddesses, warriors, and amazons greeted the eye; everywhere was beauty, everywhere the signs of unlimited wealth and Imperial grandeur.

Imperial Palaces

The scale of living in a great Roman household was so magnificent as to be almost inconceivable, and an immense army of servants was necessary to carry on its routine. It is believed that the Empress Livia had six hundred servants to wait on her personally, while the whole Imperial staff numbered several thousands.

It is at first difficult to understand how employment could be found for so many servants; but domestic duties were apportioned in a way very different from anything which exists even in the greatest royal households of modern times. The sole duty of one servant was to keep the morning dresses; another was in charge of the Imperial robe; a third kept the State robes, while many servants were employed simply as folders of clothes.

Then the toilet of a great Roman lady was a very elaborate business, necessitating the use of innumerable salves, ointments, perfumes, and cosmetics. The care of the salves and ointments was entrusted to one servant, but a separate person was required to supervise the important matter of perfumes and essences. The charge of the hot and cold water for the Empress's bath was the business of an official who had no other duties; another made it the occupation of his life to look after her shoes; and a third was given the care of her sandals. There was a governess for the pet dog, and numbers

Rome

of men and women doctors, under the supervision of a head physician, formed a necessary part of the household.

In the next chapter we will take a glance at a more modest dwelling, and see how life was lived by the ordinary citizens.

CHAPTER V

FAMILY LIFE IN OLD ROME

FOR some time after the foundation of Rome the citizens were content to dwell in mere rude huts which did little more than shelter them from the weather, and, even after these huts had been burnt down by the invading Gauls and replaced by more substantial dwellings, the houses were still badly built and inconvenient, and it was several hundred years before any great improvement was made.

In these early days a Roman house consisted of one story only, and was so small and dark that it is difficult to imagine how family life in such a dwelling can have been endurable.

But the Romans, who had no experience of a more comfortable way of living, were contented enough, and the Roman boys and girls grew up into strong, vigorous men and women, in spite of what seem to us great disadvantages.

Family Life in Old Rome

The house was entered by a vestibule, or sort of roofless porch, which led into the *ostium* or entrance-hall. The *ostium* opened directly into the *atrium*, where the family lived.

Atrium means literally a *dark room*, and though not a very cheerful or attractive name for a living-room, it was, as will be seen, not given without good reason. For the *atrium* possessed neither window nor chimney, and was lighted only by an opening in the roof. This opening served also to carry off some of the smoke from the family hearth, but we may be quite sure that enough remained in the room to cloud the atmosphere and blacken the walls.

But if the hole in the roof did not effectually let out the smoke, it did not fail to let in the rain, so it was usual to place a cistern just below it to receive and collect the water.

In the *atrium* stood the family bed; here the household work was done, meals were cooked and eaten, and the whole routine of domestic life was carried on.

The Roman matron either did her own house-work or directed her daughters or her maidservents while they did it; and when this was finished she would settle down to her spinning, that being considered the most natural occupation for a woman, and, indeed, much of the comfort of the family depended on the skill and industry of the housewife in this respect. Little Roman girls were instructed in the art from a very early age by their mothers, and to learn to spin well was for a long time looked upon as the most important part of a girl's education.

As civilization advanced, the Romans began to build themselves better and more spacious houses; separate bedrooms were added, and a dining-room or *triclinium*, as it was called, from the fact that it contained three couches, on which the diners reclined while eating.

These couches, each containing accommodation for three persons, were on a higher level than the table, and were placed round three sides of it, so that the head of each couch touched the edge of the table, and the diners could easily reach forward and take what they pleased from it.

Then, just as rich people in our own country like to have a picture-gallery, the Romans began to build picture-rooms, where the pictures, instead of hanging in frames on the wall, were painted on the sides of the room itself.

Those who had literary tastes added a book-room, and even some who did not themselves care for reading would, in order to impress their friends with their wealth and culture, have a well-stocked library, and would sometimes keep a learned man in their house to explain the contents of the books which they were unable to understand without help.

ARCH OF TITUS, BUILT A.D. 70

Family Life in Old Rome

Another improvement, which time brought into fashion, was the addition of a bath-room, though this was for a long time considered such a great luxury that it was thought wrong to take a bath on any sacred festival, and at times of national mourning even the public baths were closed.

The floors of the rooms were usually of tiles or stone, though some were mosaic, and of great beauty as to both colour and design. A very quaint mosaic floor is to be seen in the Lateran Museum, though it is more curious than beautiful, for it represents the floor of a room that requires sweeping, and is strewn with fragments of food and other trifles. Scraps of lettuce, the claw of a lobster, the skin of an apple, and similar remnants of a feast, are all wonderfully inlaid in their proper colours, and have such a natural appearance that one feels as if an energetic housemaid might really sweep them all away. Yet there they have been for many a century, and, showing no sign of age or usage, still glow just as brightly as when the floor was first laid down.

When any event of importance took place in a Roman family it was usual to make it known by placing a suitable symbol at the entrance of the house, so that visitors and passers-by might be aware of what had happened. On the occasion of a marriage a jar containing myrtle and laurel would be seen in the vestibule or *ostium;* a chaplet signified the birth of a son; while the dark, melancholy cypress was the sign of a death.

CHAPTER VI

STOLEN WIVES—A FAITHLESS DAUGHTER AND A NOBLE MOTHER

ROME, during its early days, became a kind of asylum, or city of refuge, for all sorts of desperate characters from other states; for Romulus proclaimed that any man who had offended the laws of his own country should be welcomed to the new city, and, whatever his offence might have been, should be shielded from pursuit and punishment.

This tended to increase the number of fighting-men in Rome, and so to render the Romans a more powerful nation; but the new-comers were all men, and they soon began to wish to marry and make homes for themselves in their new country.

The scarcity of women in Rome was a serious difficulty, so the Romans tried to persuade their neighbours on the Sabine Hills to give them their daughters in marriage. The Sabines, naturally enough, declined, for they loved their daughters and wished them to marry amongst their own people; besides, the Roman settlers were looked upon as rather ruffianly desperadoes, very unlikely to make good husbands.

Romulus, finding he was unable to carry his point by straightforward methods, determined to resort to craft; so he sent a friendly invitation to the Sabines, asking them to attend a festival in Rome, where all sorts of games and sports would be provided. The Sabines accepted, for, though not very kindly disposed towards their neighbours, they were attracted by the prospect of the games, and also thought they would like to see for themselves what the new city was like.

All went merrily till, at a moment when the visitors were absorbed in watching the games, a signal, previously agreed upon, was passed round, and each Roman seized a Sabine maiden in his arms, forcibly carrying her off before the eyes of her amazed and horrified family.

The Romans had won their wives, and the Sabines were obliged to retire; but their hearts were filled with bitterness and indignation at the way they had been tricked, and they did not rest till they had collected an army sufficiently strong to attack their enemies on the Palatine.

They were at first repulsed by Romulus, but the King of the Sabines continued to nourish schemes of vengeance, and specially desired to get possession of the Roman citadel on the Capitoline Hill; so he sent his soldiers to make an attempt on it. The fortress was well guarded, and the Governor, a man named Tarpeius, was faithful to his trust. Unfortunately his young daughter Tarpeia, who lived with him and knew the secrets of the fortress, was vain and fond of finery, and, in order to gratify her vanity, was tempted to commit an act of treachery which made her name infamous among the Romans for ever after. She was, as will be seen, promptly and terribly punished for her wrongdoing, for her treachery was met by equal treachery and greater cunning than her own.

The Sabine soldiers wore on their arms broad gold bracelets, which excited the envy of Tarpeia. Day by day she beheld them glittering in the sun as the soldiers moved to and fro outside the citadel, and day by day her desire to possess such splendid ornaments increased, till at last she entered into a shameful compact with the enemy to let them secretly into the fortress during the night, if each soldier would give her, as he entered, " the thing that he wore on his arm." The Sabines gladly agreed, for they were anxious above all things to obtain entrance to the citadel of the Capitol. But, though they took advantage of her baseness, they despised Tarpeia, and resolved to punish her most cruelly, and yet without breaking their promise, to the letter, at any rate. So each soldier as he passed into the citadel threw on to her the heavy shield which he wore on his arm, until the wretched girl lay crushed to death. Her body was thrown over a steep rock on the Capitoline Hill, which still bears her name, being known as the Tarpeian Rock. For a long while afterwards traitors were punished by being thrown over the Tarpeian Rock, which was looked upon as a place of evil omen.

Now it is one of the sights of Rome, and is visited by numbers of tourists, who are often disappointed with its appearance, having expected something much more imposing and terrible. It is situated in the grounds of the German Embassy, and looks peaceful enough, surrounded as it is by houses, trees, and gardens; but it is difficult for us to realize how it formerly appeared, as the ground below the rock has been raised, and a fall from the summit would not be very terrible.

But the weak and treacherous Tarpeia was no fair specimen of a Roman woman. Many stories of heroic and noble women are recorded, showing that they possessed the national virtues of courage and patriotism, and were ready to sacrifice even what they held most dear for the good of their country.

Such a woman was Volumnia, the mother of Caius Marcius, better known as Coriolanus, the name given him owing to the gallant part he played

Rome

at the taking of the town of Corioli. Coriolanus, who was a proud young Patrician, intensely desired to be chosen Consul of Rome, and used every means he could to induce the Plebeians to elect him. But he was unsuccessful, and in his mortification and disappointment became exceedingly bitter against the Plebeians who had rejected him, so, during a time of severe famine, when a cargo of grain arrived, he proposed that none should be distributed to the starving people unless they would agree to give up their right to be represented by Tribunes, who protected their liberties.

The cruelty and injustice of his proposal caused such deep and general indignation that Coriolanus was banished from Rome.

Wild with anger, he revenged himself by joining the Volscians, who were the sworn enemies of the Romans, and he undertook to lead them against Rome, knowing his own people to be at that time unprepared for war. The Romans, feeling that an attack on them at that moment would be disastrous, sent ambassadors to Coriolanus, begging him not to bring about the ruin of his country ; but he refused to listen. Then Volumnia, accompanied by his wife and children, went out to meet him and endeavour to turn him from his purpose.

She loved her son tenderly, and well knew that if he deserted his new allies they would never allow him to return to Rome alive ; but she could better endure his loss than the knowledge that by his treachery he had brought ruin to his country, so she determined, by appealing to all that was noblest and best in him, and to his love for herself, to use all her influence to save Rome, even if she must lose her son.

As soon as Coriolanus saw her he forgot for a moment all his wrongs, and remembered only the deep love and respect he had always felt for his mother. Coming towards her, he would have embraced her, but Volumnia drew back and repulsed him, saying : " Before I embrace you, tell me whether you are truly my son, or whether I see in you an enemy of Rome ? Must I blush with shame at the thought that I am your mother ? Must I weep for the day when first you saw the light ? Do you wish your mother, your wife, and these children to curse your name as that of a traitor ?"

These words melted the heart of Coriolanus and awakened his better self, and, warmly embracing his mother, he exclaimed : " Mother, you have conquered. Rome shall be saved, but you have lost your son."

His words were prophetic, for, though the Volscians, indeed, retired to their own country, they first avenged themselves on Coriolanus by putting him to death.

CHAPTER VII

THE COLOSSEUM

MOST people are familiar, from photographs or engravings, with the general form and appearance of the Colosseum; but a first sight of the actual building is, nevertheless, a surprise and a revelation ; the reality is so grand, so vast, and yet so simple, that all preconceived ideas die away, and we realize how impossible it is for pen, pencil, or camera to convey a true impression of this great pile of ruins. As once it was the very heart of Roman life, the centre of its grandeur and luxury, so it still stands supreme in interest and majesty, a splendid, though melancholy, record in stone of Rome's Imperial greatness.

From the earliest times the Romans found their chief pleasure in public games, races, sham-fights, and spectacular performances. As grace and beauty appealed to the Greeks, so did strength and splendour appeal to the Romans, and the ideal entertainment of the latter consisted of gorgeous pageantry varied by desperate combats, in which sufficient danger to life was involved to make them really exciting.

When, after the conquest of Jerusalem, Titus

THE COLOSSEUM AT SUNSET. COMMENCED A.D. 72. COMPLETED A.D. 80. *Chapter vii.*

The Colosseum

and Vespasian, laden with rich spoils, returned to Rome, the cry of the people was, " Give us cheap food and plenty of shows !" and the want of an amphitheatre large enough to gratify the public craving for amusement was felt. So twelve thousand slaves were set to work, and toiled for long weary years under relentless taskmasters at the building of the vast amphitheatre, afterwards known as the Colosseum.

The building was begun in A.D. 72, and the theatre was opened in A.D. 80, though even then it was not finished. It consisted of four stories, the three lower ones being composed of arches and columns, while the top one was a solid wall with square openings. The arches of the second and third stories were adorned with marble statues, and the wall above them was decorated with pilasters and surrounded by a cornice, into which were fixed brackets for supporting the poles of the great awning, used when necessary as a protection from the sun.

In trying to imagine how this vast building must have looked in the days of its glory, we must remember that the grey stone walls were faced with white marble, which must have had a dazzlingly beautiful effect, especially on days when the sun shone brightly and the sky was the soft intense blue of a Roman sky in fine weather.

Rome

When the theatre was opened by the Emperor Titus, games and combats of wild beasts were instituted, which went on for a hundred days, and no fewer than fifty beasts are said to have been slaughtered on the arena each day.

There was accommodation in the Colosseum for at least fifty thousand spectators, and persons of all ranks crowded eagerly to see the shows which were given on all public holidays and great occasions, and even to celebrate the funerals of important men.

The seats were carefully distributed according to rank, the most honourable being on a sort of raised terrace on the first tier. This terrace was called the *Podium*, and on occasions when there was a fashionable audience it must have been a brilliant sight, for there sat the Emperor, splendid in Imperial purple, the great State officials in their rich attire, and the beautiful group of the Vestals in their graceful, flowing dresses of spotless white. When the Empress attended the shows, it was usual for her to sit with the Vestals, who received as much respect and consideration as if they had been daughters of the Imperial family.

The second tier was occupied by men of equestrian rank; above them sat the middle-class people; and on the fourth tier were rows of wooden benches for those of the humblest rank.

Of all the vast audience, not one person was

dressed in black, for a law had been passed forbidding anyone to attend the games in black garments.

The arena consisted of a very solid wooden floor covered with sand. Underneath it were caves and cages where the wild beasts could be accommodated until they were required, and then they were introduced through trap-doors.

The combats of wild beasts were terrible and brutalizing, but much more so were the gladiatorial combats where human life was at stake and was ruthlessly sacrificed amidst the applause and frantic excitement of a crowd who seemed to possess an insatiable appetite for horrors and bloodshed.

At first the gladiators who furnished these exhibitions were drawn solely from the unhappy ranks of slaves and prisoners of war, and fought only because they were compelled to do so by their masters or conquerors, but later there arose a class of professional and voluntary gladiators, who underwent the strictest training for their calling, and only slaves and condemned criminals continued to fight on compulsion.

But, besides those who lost their lives for the sake of gain or in obedience to masters they dared not disobey, there was a more glorious band who faced death on the blood-stained arena with calm courage and even with holy joy, because of their belief that death was but the gate of life, and who counted it a small thing to lay down this mortal life in order to enter into the eternal joy of a life beyond.

The noble army of Christian martyrs who suffered in the Colosseum have left behind them memories that will outlive the story of its splendour and the record of its horrors.

CHAPTER VIII

SOME MODERN ROMAN SHOWS

In the days of Rome's Imperial greatness the favourite amusements of the people were, as we have seen, public shows or spectacular performances, and their taste for these is still as strong as it was in those old times, though they gratify it in a more harmless and less brutal manner than in the days when they crowded to the Colosseum, eager for the excitement of beholding on the arena the death-struggles of beasts and men.

The entertainment most popular with the Romans of the present day is the Cinematograph. From its first introduction it took the fancy of the populace, and the ever-increasing number of theatres and halls which are being devoted to this form of amusement in Rome proves that its popularity is still on the increase.

But though gladiatorial combats are things of the

Some Modern Roman Shows

past, the old taste for something to stir the blood and excite feelings of horror still prevails, and the most popular shows are those which exhibit pictures of terrible and tragic events and deeds of bloodshed.

The story of some of Nero's most cruel actions, and a representation of scenes from Dante's " Inferno," where the horrible sufferings of the wicked are vividly portrayed, have proved most attractive and are always sure to draw crowded houses.

But just as the bloody combats at the Colosseum were, for the sake of variety, interspersed with scenes of buffoonery or farce, the more gruesome spectacles at the Cinematograph are varied by comic scenes and interludes.

A very favourite subject for these ludicrous episodes is found in the Guardia or city police, who for some reason are not popular with the Roman people.

Whatever may be the fate of the other personages in the picture-drama, the police are always made as ridiculous as possible, and on every occasion are sure to be placed at a disadvantage. They are outwitted by the thieves they try to capture; they fall into the most obvious traps, invariably arrive on the scene of action too late to be of any use, and are, finally, left stranded in some absurd position, amidst the hearty laughter of the spectators.

The Romans are so fond of these shows that the

poorer people will often stint themselves in food in order to be able to pay the few pence necessary for entrance-money, and those who can afford it will sometimes go to two or three performances in the course of a single evening.

The Cinematograph theatres are naturally more crowded on Thursdays than on other days of the week, for the school boys and girls are then free to attend them, and, especially on a wet afternoon, they are a great resource.

On a fine day the Zoo is a still more attractive resort, being preferable to any indoor entertainment. And the Roman Zoo is, indeed, a most delightful place, for there the lions, tigers, and bears may be seen, not confined in cages, but prowling about, apparently quite at their ease, amid appropriate surroundings which have been cleverly arranged for them by means of rockwork and artificially con-structed mounds. At first sight their apparent liberty to come and go as they please is rather alarming, but there is really no danger of their pouncing on an unwary visitor and trying to make a meal of him, for, though they have the appearance of being quite free, they are, in fact, so carefully fenced in by cunningly arranged deep trenches, just too wide for them to be able to leap across, that they are as effectually secured as if they were enclosed by strong iron bars, and are certainly seen to much greater advantage. The antelopes, especially, as they leap gracefully and easily from peak to peak of the miniature crags and hills that have been provided for them, are a very pretty sight.

The Zoo has only been open for a few months, and no doubt many additions will be made to it; but even now, though the animal kingdom may not be so completely represented as it is in some other collections, a much more vivid impression is gained of the creatures when seen in movement amongst surroundings which bear at least some resemblance to their native wilds, than when one only beholds them pacing sadly backwards and forwards behind the iron bars of a cage.

CHAPTER IX

THE ROMAN FORUM AND A SPLENDID BATH-HOUSE

For several centuries after its foundation Rome could boast of none but very narrow, inconvenient streets, and, as the population increased, these were often so crowded that it was no easy task to make one's way through them. Collisions between foot-passengers were unavoidable, and frequently brought about disturbances and quarrels, which, though caused by such a trifling occurrence, sometimes developed into serious street fights. Driving in the city was still more difficult and impracticable, for hardly any of the streets were wide enough to allow a carriage to pass.

But, though the streets were narrow and dirty, the Romans were well provided with squares and parks, where they could meet for pleasure, conversation, or the transaction of business, and which formed an important part of the social life of the city. As early as the third century of the Christian era Rome possessed no fewer than eighteen public squares, or *fora*, and thirty public parks or gardens.

The most important of these *fora*, now usually spoken of as the " Forum," is also the oldest, and dates from very early Roman times. A tract of marshy ground with no buildings on it except a few sheds and huts, it was at first used only as a public market-place, but its character gradually changed as time went on. A Senate House and Court of Justice were built, and a space set apart where the citizens came to vote at election times, and in this way the Forum became the centre of the chief social and political interests of the city.

The old Senate House was a plain bare structure, containing a wooden tribunal and rows of plain wooden benches for the accommodation of the senators, who were quite satisfied with their frugal surroundings, for they would have thought it unworthy of their high office to trouble themselves about bodily comfort. They were, indeed, so opposed to self-indulgence that they would not permit their hall to be heated, even in the coldest weather. There is a story that on one occasion the cold was so intense that they were fairly frozen out, and, though engaged in discussing an important matter, were obliged hurriedly to disperse, thus exposing themselves to the gibes and jeers of the populace, always ready, in ancient as in modern Rome, with light-hearted raillery for the small misfortunes of others.

Under the Emperors the Forum was greatly extended. Fire and time did their work on the old buildings, and new and more splendid ones took their place. Temples, public buildings, triumphal arches, and statuary were raised, until the Forum became crowded with stately monuments. But of all these there now remain only fragmentary ruins, many of which are difficult even to identify with any certainty. It would be impossible here to attempt a description of even the chief monuments of the Forum, but there are two whose very names are interesting, for one carries our thoughts back to the very foundation of Rome, and the other fascinates the imagination because it is connected with that mysterious order of the Vestal Virgins of which we have heard so much, but of whose inner life and history we know so little.

The so-called tomb of Romulus was discovered only about twelve years ago, when, during some excavations, an immense black pavement of a rare kind of marble came to light. There had always been a tradition that Romulus was buried on the spot where this great marble slab was found, and it had been recorded by an ancient writer that the tomb was adorned with two sculptured lions. At a little distance from the marble slab an inscription was found which was very difficult to decipher, as it dated from about 500 B.C., but it is now generally accepted as referring to the spot where it was discovered. It speaks of it as a very sacred place, and mentions feasts and sacrifices as having been held there, and finally threatens anyone who shall violate this sacred spot with death from the hands of the gods. The two sculptured lions are still un-discovered, so there is no positive proof that this was actually the tomb of the founder of Rome ; but there is sufficient probability that it was so to make it a monument of rare interest.

The House of the Vestals stood at the foot of the Palatine Hill, and when its ruins were discovered, in 1883, it was possible to distinguish the parts of the house which were used for official purposes from those where the Sisterhood spent their hours of

The Roman Forum

privacy, and where the domestic life of the house was carried on. Many statues of Vestals, some very beautiful, and also inscriptions bearing witness to the shining virtues of some of the Sisters, were found. But the secrets of their Order, which had never been revealed from the beginning of Rome to the fall of the Empire, died with them, for not a trace of anything referring to them has been found. In another chapter we shall hear more about the Vestals, but now we will leave the Forum, and take a glance at an ancient Roman bath-house, which, as you will see, was an institution of great importance.

The remains of the great bathing establishments of Rome form a very interesting study, and give us a vivid idea of the habits and customs of Imperial times ; for, though the luxurious appointments of the days of their prosperity are swept away, and the crowd of elegant young men and women of fashion who frequented them are replaced by bustling groups of tourists or by desolation and solitude, there is enough left of their original structures to show us how spacious and commodious these must have been, and to enable us to form some sort of picture, though perhaps an inadequate one, of the scenes witnessed long ago by these gaunt, bare walls and echoing chambers in the days of their glory.

The ruins of the Baths of Caracalla, on the Appian

Rome

Way, are the most extensive in Rome, except those of the Colosseum. These baths were so large that 1,600 bathers could be accommodated at the same time. At certain hours they were open to people of all ranks ; children were allowed to bathe without payment, and the poorest plebeian could, at the cost of a small copper coin, enjoy a bath equal in luxury to that of the greatest monarch. A marble chair was provided for each bather, hot water poured from the walls into the marble basins in a never-failing stream through solid silver spouts, and the walls themselves were adorned with beautiful and curious mosaics in rich glowing colours. Underground passages were provided, through which the attendants could pass without disturbing the bathers, and appear promptly when required with the cosmetics and hot towels, which were regarded as simple necessaries by these luxurious people.

But the Bath-house served many other purposes and offered many other attractions besides the pleasure of bathing. There were lovely gardens in which groups of friends might often be seen strolling, laughing, talking, exchanging the latest gossip of the day, or perhaps listening to a fashionable poet reciting a new poem : for it was not at all unusual for a poet to submit his verses to the criticism of the world of fashion, and nowhere could he find a better opportunity of doing so than at the baths.

Then there was a restaurant, where choice meals were served; all necessary appliances were provided for games and gymnastics, and an excellent library supplied books and news-sheets.

In short, the young Roman of Imperial times found at the baths all, and more, than a Londoner of the twentieth century can find in the most luxurious club. But there is no doubt that this refinement of luxury, and the temptation offered by these resorts to rich young men to wile away most of the day in a sort of busy idleness, did much to undermine the stern virtues of the ancient Roman character, and so to bring about the decay of a great empire.

CHAPTER X

A SISTERHOOD OF SIX

THE order of the Vestals consisted of only six members, and no new member could be admitted except on the death or retirement of one of the six. When it was necessary to choose a new one, there was zealous competition for the honour amongst the parents of girls who might be eligible; but it was no easy matter for even people of power and influence to secure for their child admission into the charmed circle.

To stand any chance of being chosen, a girl must be between six and ten years old, of perfect beauty,

Rome

and free from the smallest physical defect—a lisp, a stammer, or a squint being sufficient to disqualify her. Her parents must both be alive, of spotless reputation, and be able to prove that they had always lived together in complete harmony.

When a candidate had been accepted, she was taken to the House of the Vestals, where her hair was cut off, and she was clothed in the pure white robes of the order.

It was the law that every Vestal should serve the goddess Vesta for thirty years, and during this period she was bound by solemn vows to obey the rules of the Order in every particular; to abstain from marriage, and to devote herself to her duties in the temple, where the sacred fire was kept. For the first ten years she was a novice, and had to learn her duties, and during her novitiate was called by the name of Amata, or the "beloved one." The following ten years were spent in the performance of the rites she had been taught, and after this she became an instructress of the younger Vestals. At the end of the thirty years she might, if she chose, either retire or marry, but it was seldom that a Vestal took advantage of this liberty.

For one thing, there was a strong popular feeling that it was unlucky for one who had been consecrated to the service of Vesta to marry, and for another she enjoyed greater wealth, power, and

A Sisterhood of Six

consideration as a Vestal than she could possibly have had as a married woman. The Order was very wealthy, and its members possessed rights and privileges that were granted to no other Roman woman.

As soon as a girl entered the Order, she became quite independent of the authority of her parents, and had the right to make her own will and dispose of her property as she liked. She was allowed to drive through the streets in a carriage, while other women, even the most wealthy, were usually obliged to content themselves with being carried in a sort of sedan-chair.

When a Vestal drove out, everyone had to make way for her carriage and if by chance she encountered a criminal being led to his death, he was at once pardoned and set free.

Strict secrecy was preserved regarding the inner life of the Sisterhood, and even when the Order came to an end nothing was found to disperse the atmosphere of mystery which has always surrounded their memory.

We know, however, that they inspired the deepest respect and confidence ; that important State papers, and sometimes the wills of the Emperors and other powerful people, were placed in their care ; that State secrets were confided to them ; and that they were consulted on matters of the greatest public importance.

Rome

Such were the glories of the Order ; but there is a darker side to the picture, for, if their privileges were great, so also were the penalties which they had to pay in the rare cases where they failed to keep their vows.

If a Vestal failed in her duty at the temple she was severely punished ; and if she broke her vow to abstain from marriage, she was condemned to pay the penalty with her life, and that in a most cruel manner, by being buried alive.

The condemnation and execution of a Vestal was, fortunately, a very rare event, but when it occurred, even the Romans, who could behold, not only without shrinking, but even with cynical enjoyment, the cruel sufferings of man and beast in the arena of the Colosseum, were shaken with horror and compunction.

CHAPTER XI

THE LARGEST CHURCH AND THE GREATEST PALACE IN THE WORLD

THE world-famous Church of St. Peter is chiefly remarkable for its great size and magnificent proportions, for, though it contains many imposing and costly monuments, only a few of these possess any real beauty.

THE BRONZE STATUE OF ST PETER IN THE
CHURCH OF ST PETER. *Page 50*

The Largest Church in the World

The great open space in front of the church is surrounded by colonnades, and the chief entrance, with its finely sculptured, brazen doors, is approached by a flight of steps, so wide and large that men and women going up or down them look from a little distance hardly more important than flies.

As soon as a visitor enters the square, he is accosted by men and boys selling picture-postcards or cheap mosaic jewellery ; a polite refusal to buy has no effect, for these persevering hawkers continue to offer their wares in most persuasive tones, rapidly reducing their prices, until as the tourist reaches the entrance, the postcards at first offered as " very sheep " at a halfpenny each, are pressed upon him at the moderate price of ten a penny.

Once inside the church, all is quietness and solemnity, and as one stands in the great nave, looking towards the tomb of St. Peter, with its innumerable glimmering lights which burn perpetually, or beneath the dome, with its 400 feet of height, one cannot fail to be deeply impressed by the dignity and grandeur of this largest church in the world.

The beautiful form and exquisite symmetry of the dome are due to Michelangelo, whom many people consider the greatest artist that Italy has ever produced.

The finest monument in the church is also his

work, and represents the Madonna, seated, and supporting the dead body of our Lord on her knees. It is of white marble, and the figures, which are very beautiful in their simple dignity and pathos, are life-size.

In the right aisle there is a stately bronze statue of St. Peter, who is represented sitting in a throne-like chair, with the right hand raised as if in blessing. This statue is very ancient, but its origin is not clearly known. It is an object of special veneration to the Romans, and on Sundays or festival days many of the poorer inhabitants of the city, and numbers of peasants from the neighbouring villages, make a sort of humble pilgrimage to the Cathedral to show their reverence for the patron saint of Rome. Men and women of all ages draw near one after another, and, after kneeling for a moment in prayer, reverently imprint a kiss on the right foot of the statue and pass on. Even toddling children and babies are lifted up that they, too, may pay their homage to the saint; and this stream of worshippers has been so constant that the solid bronze of the foot is considerably worn away by the kisses of the faithful.

On the great festivals of the Church the services at St. Peter's are as grand as rich vestments and a splendid ceremonial can make them; but the crowd of not always reverent sight-seers is so great that the church is much less solemn and impressive at such times than in quieter seasons.

Side by side with the largest church in the world stands the greatest palace. The Vatican, which for over five hundred years has been the residence of the Popes, is so vast that it seems impossible to ascertain with certainty how many rooms, halls, galleries, and chapels it contains, the estimates given at different times varying from one to eleven thousand. The truth probably lies somewhere between these two extremes. The palace, with its court-yards, outbuildings, etc., covers more than thirteen acres of ground, and contains countless art treasures and antiquities, so that it is impossible to compute the enormous amount of wealth represented within its walls.

The most beautiful chapel in the Vatican is known as the Sistine, having been erected by Pope Sixtus IV. towards the end of the fifteenth century, and its painted ceiling is the greatest work contained in this great treasure-house of art and beauty.

The story of the painting of this ceiling is a story of heroic work pursued under the greatest difficulties, and reveals to us, not only the supreme genius of the painter, but his unflagging perseverance and undaunted courage.

For nearly six years the great artist, Michel-angelo, laboured incessantly, mounted on a high scaffolding, and obliged to paint lying on his back.

We may form some idea of the fatigue he endured from a letter written by him to a friend when he was nearing the end of his task, in which he says: "I have become so cramped that I think I have forgotten how to stand upright, so do not be surprised when you see me to find that I am a bent old man no longer able to raise my head and look up at the sky!" This letter is written in a half-joking spirit, and must not be taken literally; but the fact remains that he had sacrificed health, energy, ease, and pleasure for six long years in order to devote himself entirely to his great work.

For he regarded his genius as a gift from God, to be faithfully employed in His service, and, in his consistent pursuit of what was highest and best in art, he strove to render a faithful account of the talents entrusted to him.

Next in interest to the Sistine Chapel are the State apartments, where the frescoes of Raphael are to be seen. Pope Julius II. had entrusted the decoration of these rooms to several painters, who began the work, and were afterwards joined by Raphael, who was then quite young, but who soon gave proof of such brilliant talent that the whole of the work was confided to him. Unfortunately, his early death prevented him from completing it, but though the decoration of these stately rooms was neither begun nor finished by him, his work is so much the finest there that they are always spoken of as the " Raphael Rooms," for it is he who has made them famous.

CHAPTER XII

COUNTRY HOUSES

As the wealth of the Romans increased, they became more and more luxurious in their way of living. All the nobles, and those of the citizens who were rich enough, began to build themselves villas on the Campagna, as the great undulating plain which surrounds Rome is called, and in these country houses they would spend the summer months, so as to avoid the stifling heat and noisy crowded streets of the city. They vied with each other in the splendour and beauty of their villas, and as time went on it became the fashion to have more than one country house, so that many a great noble would build himself several in different parts of the Campagna, and was able to travel from one to another over a large extent of country without ever leaving his own property.

The Campagna was not at all a healthy region, being frequently ravaged by fever ; indeed, when we read the accounts given by ancient writers of the

terrible epidemics which from time to time des-
cended on the inhabitants, sometimes sweeping away
whole families, and always leaving great desolation
and distress, it seems strange that the Romans did
not seek some more distant but healthier part of the
country for their summer residences.

But the difficulties of travelling were so great,
and the roads so infested by bands of robbers, that
the nearness of the Campagna to the city outweighed
all other considerations. As an example of the
dangerous state of the roads, we read that a certain
schoolmaster who was walking with his boys on
the Via Campana was attacked by highwaymen, and
murdered, with seven of his pupils. Bearing in
mind that not only one, but many such incidents
probably occurred, even in the unprotected country
roads in the neighbourhood of Rome, it is not surprising that the Romans did not care to undertake
the difficulties and dangers of a long journey through
lonely country, but continued to build their villas
on their own Campagna, which gradually became
a sort of vast park, dotted with beautiful country
houses surrounded by pleasure grounds.

In gardening the Romans seem to have preferred
art to Nature, for hardly a tree was allowed to grow
in its own natural way, but nearly all were cut and
clipped and distorted into various strange shapes,
generally those of animals or birds, and the greatest

triumph of the gardener's skill was to make a tree look as unlike a tree as possible, and as nearly like a lion or an eagle as he could.

Very few flowers were cultivated, with the exception of violets and roses, but of these there were a great many, as they flourished and grew luxuriantly on the soil of the Campagna.

Fountains and statues adorned these formal gardens; there were shady alleys for a quiet stroll, and litters were at hand for those who were not inclined for exertion, and preferred to make their tour of the grounds borne by slaves, of whom there were always plenty in attendance. Indeed, the position occupied in fashionable society by a Roman in the days of Rome's prosperity largely depended on the number of slaves he owned, and one of the first questions asked when seeking information about a new acquaintance was sure to be : " How many slaves does he keep ?" If the answer were satisfactory, the new-comer would be well received, but if not, only a condescending welcome would be given him, from which we may gather that snobbishness, if not quite as old as the hills, is certainly as old as Imperial Rome.

In the grounds belonging to a fine Roman villa there was usually a hippodrome, or circus, for horse-exercise, racing, and other games, where the young men of the family and their friends could find plenty of amusement, so that they had no reason to fear the dullness of country life.

But of all this smiling park-land there now remains little more than a sweep of open and rather desolate country, almost bare of trees, where the song of a bird is hardly ever heard, and through which one may walk for miles without coming across any human habitation above the rank of a humble farmhouse, or meeting any human being but a lonely shepherd in charge of his flock. Here and there, it is true, the ruins of some once lovely villa, or the crumbling walls of some ancient tomb, serve to remind us of the wealth and splendour of the past.

One reason why the note of a bird is so seldom heard on the Campagna is the scarcity of trees, but there is another and a sadder reason for this silence —namely, that in Italy song-birds are constantly being shot down by the peasants and poorer people, who use them as food, with the result that they are yearly decreasing in number. The extreme poverty of the people is their only excuse for such barbarism ; but it is no doubt a strong temptation to them to be able to procure a meal which costs nothing, or next to nothing, for the sum charged for a licence to shoot is so trifling that even the very poor contrive to pay it.

A LITTLE GLEANER IN THE CAMPAGNA. *Page 56*

CHAPTER XIII

SOME INTERESTING ROMAN TOMBS

THE tombs and monuments erected long ago by the Romans in honour of their dead are not only of great interest, but have proved most valuable to all students of ancient Roman life and history, for their inscriptions often throw light on the daily life and customs of the people, while from the sculptures and carvings which decorate many of the tombs, information may be gathered as to the way in which certain handicrafts and trades were carried on. As an instance of a monument which gives some insight into the practical life of those early days may be mentioned the tomb of a rich baker named Eurysaces, supposed to date from about 50 B.C. It stands just outside one of the city gates (Porta Maggiore), and, though not exactly beautiful in shape or design, it is well worth a careful examination. It would seem that Eurysaces was proud of being a baker, for the decorations he chose for his tomb were all illustrative of his trade. The lower part of the monument is plain and solid-looking, but the upper part is decorated by three rows of round kneading-troughs such as were used by bakers of those times, and above these there is a frieze of roughly sculptured scenes, showing the bringing in and grinding of the wheat, the placing of the fire in the oven, the process of bread-making, the weighing of the bread, and the distribution of the loaves.

Round the space between the decorated upper part and the plain basement, the following inscription is engraved, and, though the spelling leaves something to be desired, the meaning is sufficiently clear :

" This is the tomb of M. V. Eurysaces the baker, contractor for supplying bread to the servants of the magistrates of Rome."

It is supposed that the tomb of the wife of Eury-saces stood near that of her husband, but all that now remains of it is a part of the inscription, signi-fying : " Atista was my wife ; she was when alive the best of women, the remains of whose body are in this bread-basket."

Besides tombs raised to the honour of individuals, there were great burial-places for the poor, and large tombs, called *columbaria*, built to accommo-date many coffins or urns, for the Romans some-times buried and sometimes burned the bodies of their dead ; in the latter case the ashes were depo-sited in small urns, which were placed in niches round the walls of the family tomb. The name *colum-barium* means a pigeon-house, and was adopted be-cause the niches for the urns resembled pigeon-holes.

Some Interesting Roman Tombs

Sometimes a man of high rank, who employed many servants, provided a *columbarium* for them, as well as for his own family, and in some cases the servants were allowed the privilege of burying their near relations also in the *columbarium* of their master.

The humbler inhabitants, who had no wealth to leave behind them, and could not afford to prepare a costly family tomb, were none the less anxious to ensure decent burial for themselves and their belongings, and, with this end in view, a number of men serving one master, or having some other interest in common, would club together to build a *columbarium*, each owning a certain share, and being able to leave the niches to which he had a claim to his children or heirs, just as he might leave a house, furniture, or any other property.

During some excavations on the Campagna a family tomb was discovered which had remained sealed and undisturbed for nearly eighteen centuries. The interior was an ordinary-looking room with whitewashed walls, and contained several tombs without inscriptions ; but in the middle of the chamber stood a beautifully carved block of marble, with a Latin inscription meaning : " To the soul of Minicia Marcella, daughter of Fundanus ; died at the age of 12 years, 11 months, and 7 days." This young girl, whose short life ended so many centuries ago, seems to have been a remarkable and beautiful character, with many of the noblest qualities of a Roman patrician maiden, for Professor Lanciani, who was present at the opening of her tomb, tells us that she was undoubtedly the same Minicia Marcella about whom the author, Pliny the Younger, says in a letter to a friend, written soon after her death; " I write to you with my soul deeply saddened and distressed on account of the death of the younger daughter of our Fundanus, a bright, lovable, and attractive girl, worthy not only of a longer life, but I might almost say of immortality. Although she had not yet completed her thirteenth year, she united the wisdom and gravity of a matron to the simplicity and gentleness of a girl, the modesty and sweetness of a virgin. With what tranquillity, patience, and strength of mind she supported her fatal disease, followed the advice of the attending physicians, consoled her father and elder sister, and maintained the declining strength of her body with the vigour of her mind !"

The virtues and talents of another child, Quintus Sulpicius Maximus, who died in the reign of Domitian, are touchingly recorded on a tablet taken from his tomb, and now preserved in the Palace of the Conservators on the Capitol. This boy must certainly have differed quite as much from most little boys of his age as Minicia Marcella did from an ordinary girl of twelve or thirteen, for, after giving a description of his great ability and intellectual promise, which made him the object of much love and many hopes, the epitaph concludes by telling us that, owing to his too great application and industry, he died at the age of eleven years from overwork !

CHAPTER XIV

ORACLES AND INVALIDS

IT is not surprising that the wealthier citizens of Rome were glad to escape from the crowded city into fresher air during the summer months, for though in the Campagna, as we have seen, fever was very prevalent, violent outbreaks were only occasional, and there were sometimes long intervals between them ; in any case, the occupants of the villas often escaped infection, even when the poorer people in the little farms and villages were suffering and dying in great numbers. In Rome itself, for long after its foundation, the conditions of life were so insanitary that, instead of feeling any surprise at the number of deaths that occurred when an epidemic visited the city, we are more inclined to wonder that the Romans were on the whole such a strong, vigorous people.

Decaying animal and vegetable refuse poisoned the air in the streets, and, till the building of the aqueducts brought pure water from a distance, the people were dependent on the tainted water of the Tiber, which they habitually drank, in spite of the fact that it was polluted by the drainage of the city, as well as in many other ways.

The Romans did not for a long time realize the importance of taking practical measures to make their city a more healthy place, because they considered any general sickness to be a visitation of the gods rather than the result of unhealthy surroundings. Their first idea was, therefore, to conciliate the angry deities, and induce them to remove the evil. But in order to propitiate the gods, it was necessary to find out if possible what particular honours would be most acceptable to them, and for this purpose the oracles would be consulted, and their counsel followed. If the sickness abated and disappeared, the public faith was increased and confirmed, but if no good result seemed likely to follow, it was thought that the oracles had been misunderstood, for, as is well known, oracular utterances may usually be interpreted in more ways than one.

Sometimes the Sibylline Books were consulted, and the Augurs were called in to interpret them. These Sibylline Books, to which the Romans appealed not only in times of sickness, but on other occasions of public danger or difficulty, were believed to have been bought by King Tarquin the Proud from a mysterious old Sibyl or Wise Woman, who appeared before him one day offering for sale nine volumes, for which she asked a great price, but refused to allow him to examine the contents of the books before purchasing them. Under these circumstances the King not unnaturally refused to buy, and the old woman withdrew in anger. A little later, having destroyed three of the books, she returned with the remainder, and again, still demanding the same high price, she asked the King to buy. A second, time he refused, thinking the old woman must be mad ; but when she returned once again, this time with only three volumes, for which she still asked the same sum as before, Tarquin began to think there was some deep mystery connected with the books, and made up his mind to purchase them. The Sibyl disappeared at once and for ever, and the Augurs were called in to examine the mysterious volumes. They did not disclose what was in the books, but declared them to be filled with words of oracular wisdom, at the same time advising that they should be most carefully guarded, as the fortunes and prosperity of Rome might depend on their safe keeping. So they were placed in the Capitol, and only the Augurs were allowed access to them.

At one time, when a great plague was raging, the

Rome

Sibylline Books were consulted, and the Augurs declared that they directed the removal of the god Æsculapius from Epidaurus to Rome as the surest means of stopping the pestilence. In accordance with this advice the god was brought with great care and respect to the plague-stricken city, and installed in a temple, which soon became the scene of many strange practices. The more ignorant of the people would bring any relation or friend afflicted by severe illness, and lay him in the outer room of the sanctuary, where a sleeping-draught would be administered to him in the confident belief that Æsculapius would reveal to the patient in a dream what must be done in order to cure him. The directions given by the god were often very curious, and did not seem at all likely to benefit any invalid; but whatever they were, the priests of the temple undertook to carry them out, and when, as sometimes happened, the patient recovered, great was the honour paid to Æsculapius.

Another strange way of treating illness practised by the Romans was to take the sufferer into some public place in the city, where he would remain for some hours in full view of all the passers-by. The latter would stop and examine the patient, ask any question that occurred to them about his symptoms, and then offer their advice as to the best means of treating his illness. In some cases the invalid was

A CARDINAL IN THE GARDEN OF A ROMAN VILLA

allowed to choose the cure he liked best, but in others the zealous friends tried one suggestion after another in the hope that if one did not succeed another might. All things considered, it is hardly surprising that deaths were numerous and cures comparatively rare.

Even in the present day many of the poor people of Rome are much more inclined to seek the help of a *strega*, or witch, when they are ill than that of an orthodox doctor, and it is pitiful to think of the blind credulity with which they part with money they can ill spare in return for nostrums that often have a bad effect, or charms which, naturally, have no effect at all.

It is strange, indeed, that faith in the power of the *strega* still survives in spite of the gradual spread of education and enlightenment amongst the populace, but there is no doubt that she still has a following among the more ignorant and superstitious of the people of Rome.

CHAPTER XV

THE CATACOMBS

As the progress of Christianity advanced the Christians in Rome naturally desired to have burial-places of their own, where they could give Christian burial to their dead, and so they began to build for

Rome

themselves those wonderful labyrinthine tombs which in modern times came to be called the Catacombs, though the name given to them by the Early Christians was *Cæmetaria,* which means " places of rest." They consisted at first of single underground passages a few feet in width, with niches at the side, each of sufficient size to accommodate a human body, or in some cases for two to be laid side by side, and were dimly lighted from above by a hole in the ground. But in course of time the passages were excavated one above another till there were four or five stories of them, then, as space became more precious, family tombs were turned into public cemeteries, and these were sometimes connected with one another till the narrow passages with their silent occupants covered hundreds of miles, forming a sort of city of the dead outside, and almost encircling, the walls of Rome. For it was against the Roman law for a dead body, or even an urn containing its ashes, to be buried within the city walls. In times of persecution the Catacombs were used by the Christians as places of refuge from their enemies, where they might perform the sacred rites of their religion secretly and unmolested.

Among the most ancient and interesting of the Catacombs are those of St. Agnes, outside the gate of the city known as the Porta Pia.

The Catacombs

The steps by which we enter are said to be those originally placed there in the time of Constantine, and dates are found on some of the tombs which show that interments were made in the first gallery as early as A.D. 336.

Among the most striking features of these Catacombs are the two chambers hewn out of the rock, which were used as a school for instructing young people in the Christian faith. The room used for youths has an arm-chair of carved stone on either side of the entrance, but even in those early days the school buildings for girls were not so handsome as those for boys, and the room used for the maidens contains only plain seats. Opening out of the gallery is another room, which seems to have been used as a chapel, and which contains some curious paintings of scenes from the Old and New Testaments.

Beside many of the tombs various symbols are scratched in the mortar—palms to indicate victory over death, anchors signifying hope, doves which were symbolical of the human soul freed from the trammels of the body, and many others, each containing some hidden meaning. Here and there we find a rude tracing of the figure of the Good Shepherd, which seems to have been the subject best loved by the early Christians, as it is invariably met with wherever the Christians worshipped or buried their dead.

Rome

The child-saint to whom these Catacombs were dedicated was martyred at the age of twelve under the Emperor Diocletian. The story of her life has always been a great favourite with the Romans, and has been very fully related by many writers, ancient and modern. It is, of course, difficult to tell how far these accounts are accurate in detail, but it cannot be doubted that the child-martyr's pure and holy life, so soon and so cruelly cut short, has left behind it a strong influence for good, and that she still stands forth as a bright ideal of purity and faithfulness to many a poor ignorant Roman girl.

We are told that she was a child of great beauty, and that her disposition was as lovely as her outward form, for she had loved Christ from her infancy, and was filled with all spiritual gifts. Her courage and firmness were so great that neither the fear of a cruel death, nor the temptations of a wealthy and luxurious life which was offered her, could make her swerve from her strong, childlike faith. When her tormentors found that nothing could induce her to renounce Christianity, or even to waver in her confession of faith, she was condemned to death, and suffered martyrdom, with perfect calmness, and even joy, in her thirteenth year.

But, though her persecutors could put her to death, they could not destroy her memory and her influence, and she is still remembered with love and veneration.

When the Princess Constantia, daughter of the Emperor Constantine, was attacked by the terrible disease of leprosy, she retired to the tomb of Agnes to pray for relief from her sufferings, and while she was praying fervently she heard a voice saying to her : "Arise, Constantia, and go on constantly in the faith of Christ, who shall heal your disease." The voice sounded to her like the voice of Agnes, for whom she had a special love, and when, soon afterwards, she was cured of her leprosy, she was so full of gratitude that she persuaded her father, as a thankoffering, to build a church above the Catacombs where lay the body of St. Agnes, and to dedicate it to her.

CHAPTER XVI

ROMAN SCHOOLBOYS

THE Roman schoolboy is in many ways very like his English brother—that is to say, he does not as a rule work more than he is obliged; he is fond of play, loves anything which contains a spice of mischief or adventure, and has a great capacity for hero-worship.

He has perhaps faults with which the English schoolboy cannot be charged; but, on the other hand, he is happily free from some of his weaknesses.

Rome

In the first place, the Roman boy is entirely exempt from the vice of snobbishness, and it would never enter his head that his behaviour to a schoolfellow could be influenced by the worldly position or wealth of the parents of his companion, nor that he himself will be less valued by his friends if his father should chance to be a poor man. He will give the most willing allegiance and devotion to the friend whom he admires and loves, and will follow his lead with unquestioning loyalty; but this hero-worship is for something in the boy himself, not for anything in his circumstances. Among Roman schoolboys the question " Who is he ?" is very seldom asked, but the question " What is he ?" is considered all-important.

On some points they show themselves to be more intelligent and less the victims of prejudice than the average British boy ; for instance, if they happen to be learning English they will take a good deal of trouble to speak it with a correct accent, and would find it very difficult to understand the feeling of many an English schoolboy, who, being reluctantly compelled by circumstances to imbibe some knowledge of the French language, seems to consider it beneath his dignity, and even rather affected and effeminate, to attempt to speak it after the manner of the natives, but prefers to retain a sturdy and uncompromising British accent. On the other hand, their code of schoolboy honour is less strict than ours, and tale-bearing is not so uncommon nor so absolutely condemned as it is in our own schools. In a fight there is not much idea of fair play, but each combatant will without scruple make use of all the weapons with which Nature has endowed him, though an Italian boy will sometimes be moved by passionate indignation at the sight of cruelty or oppression on the part of a big boy towards a little one, and will fly to the defence of the latter, when an English boy would pass by on the other side, with the reflection that, after all, it was no business of his. There is very little bullying in Italian schools, and the ragging of a new boy, for the simple reason that he is new, is a form of humour almost unknown.

The holidays at Christmas and Easter are very short, only four, or at most five, days being the ordinary allowance, but the summer holidays are of a generous length, for after the second week in July the heat is usually too great for much energetic work to be done, so the schools are closed from then until the first week in October. During term-time Thursday, and not Saturday, is the weekly holiday, and on this day wherever one goes in Rome school-boys seem to abound. For their holiday is not, as a matter of course, devoted to outdoor sports, and they are usually to be seen at the Cinematograph, or

Rome

driving or walking with their parents, while at the cafés and confectioners' shops they are in great force, showing keen appreciation of the coffee and whipped cream, and the various tempting and delicious cakes for which Rome is famous.

In many of the schools the boys wear a neat dark uniform, with black kid gloves, and may often be met in this very correct attire walking in an orderly "crocodile" through the streets. The ordinary costume of the schoolboy who does not wear a uniform consists of a short jacket, floppy loose knickerbockers, and *short* socks, and is worn even by boys of fifteen or sixteen who have almost attained their full growth. Their appearance to English eyes is certainly rather comical at first, but Italians, fortunately for themselves, are very free from self-consciousness, and they walk about quite happily in a costume which no self-respecting Briton above the age of five would consent to wear.

A characteristic which the Roman boy shares with the boys of all other parts of the world, but which seems in him to be almost abnormally developed, is his mania for scribbling his own name or that of his special friend or enemy, with crude remarks of a personal description, in forbidden and unsuitable places. Surrounded as he is by beautiful monuments in stone and marble, he has no idea of respecting them, and there is hardly a statue or monument

in the public parks or streets of Rome which does not bear ample witness to his vandalism.

In this respect the Roman boy has not changed much since the days of the Cæsars, for his handiwork may still be seen on the walls of ruined palaces or the bases of mutilated statues which have been brought to light in modern times, after lying buried and out of sight for many ages. On the Palatine Hill there is a ruined building, now known as the School of the Pages, which contains, scratched on its walls, some records of schoolboy wit and humour, to which antiquity gives an interest they would not otherwise possess. It is supposed, though not certain, that this house was used as a training-school for Imperial pages, who were promoted from a school in the neighbourhood to the pleasanter conditions and greater freedom they enjoyed during their preparation for Court life. The inscriptions are not complimentary to their former teacher, who seems to have been a hard taskmaster, for most of them are frank expressions of the writer's delight at having escaped from his old school and all its hardships. One of the boys, more ambitious than the rest, had scratched on the wall a rude drawing of an ass turning a mill, with the words : " Labour, O little ass, as I have laboured, and you, too, shall be rewarded."

Rome

CHAPTER XVII

POPULAR ROMAN GAMES

THOUGH games and sports do not form an important part of the school-life of a Roman boy, it must not be supposed that therefore the Romans do not play games, or even that they are at all indifferent about them. They have their own sports, on which they are quite as keen as any English boy is on cricket or football, and they specially excel in games requiring strength and agility combined.

The game of *pallone*, which is to Italy what cricket is to England, is one of these, and can only be well played by a strong athletic boy or quite young man, for it demands so much more quickness and agility than cricket that it has to be given up much earlier in life. *Pallone*, which, under the name of *pila*, was played by the youths of ancient Rome and probably long before their time, may be the common ancestor of cricket, football, and tennis, for it combines elements of all three games.

The players are divided into sides of any number from five to eight, the ground being marked out in the form of an oblong, with a dividing line across the centre, and looks something like a tennis-court without a net. The ball is made of leather, and is

74

Popular Roman Games

about the size of a cricket-ball. It is heavier than one would expect, though it is not solid, but inflated with air like a football. This has to be done by machinery, in order to render it quite hard and unyielding.

The batsmen, as we must call them for want of a better word, do not use bats, but wear on the right hand a sort of wooden gauntlet, with which they strike the ball. The latter, should a player be clumsy enough to receive it on his arm instead of with his gauntlet, is not heavy enough to inflict a very serious injury, but, when driven with great force, it can inflict a nasty bruise, and there are even occasional records of a broken bone, though this is a rare occurrence.

At one end of the ground there is a little platform, and on this the best batsmen takes his place, the others being stationed at different points, so as to cover as far as possible the ground to be guarded by their side.

When the chief batsman has received the first ball, which is served by the leading player on the other side, the play becomes general, the ball being struck as in tennis, by the player who is most advantageously placed for taking it. The ball may be taken at a volley or on the rebound, and long rallies of a most exciting kind often take place. The number of players on each side, and the graceful swiftness and agility with which they dart from point to point of the court, renders a long rally in *pallone* an exceedingly pretty, as well as exciting, spectacle. Every good stroke is greeted by the applause of the spectators, and any player who succeeds in saving a point for his side several times in succession by a well-directed stroke receives an enthusiastic ovation.

Another game very popular with the Romans, though much less exciting than *pallone*, is *boccette*, in which any number of players may take part. This game a good deal resembles bowls, though instead of the smooth velvety green, an ordinary piece of rough ground is chosen, and a great deal of variety is given to the game by the irregularities of the surface, as it is difficult for even a very skilful player to calculate the effect of these obstacles on the course of his ball.

Campana, which is the Roman equivalent for hopscotch, is a great favourite with both girls and boys, and is played in the streets wherever a few feet of space is available.

The game of *morra*, which requires neither apparatus nor space, as it is played simply with the fingers, is so ancient that its origin is lost in obscurity, but there is evidence that it was played by the Egyptians two thousand years before the Christian era. The method of playing the game is very simple. Two players stand opposite each other, and when, at a given signal, the play begins each simultaneously raises his hand in front of him, holding up one or more of his fingers, and at the same time calling out what he guesses to be the total number of fingers shown by himself and his adversary. If one player only guesses right he scores a point, but, of course, if both are right or both wrong, or there has been any irregularity in the play, nothing is scored. The game is played very rapidly, and it is always necessary for a third person to act as umpire and keep the score.

Morra was formerly so popular in Rome that it was to be seen (and heard) being played at all times and seasons, and in every part of the city—at street-corners, outside taverns, under archways, on the cab-rank; in short, anywhere and everywhere. It was never played for love, but the stake was more often a flask of wine than money. The opportunities of cheating were so many and so tempting that street quarrels between players became a serious disturbance to the peace of the city. These disputes often resulted in bloodshed, and sometimes even in death, so the Government wisely decided to interfere, and a law was passed making it a legal offence to play *morra* in the streets of Rome.

Unfortunately the game still remains popular amongst the Roman people, who often manage to evade the law, and are wont in fine weather to repair during their spare time to some little tavern just outside the gates of the city, where they may enjoy their beloved pastime undisturbed.

The game of knuckle-bones is also of very ancient origin, and has been popular amongst the Roman girls and boys from the earliest days of the city up to the present time, and its popularity shows no sign of waning. It is interesting to see how the children in the poorer parts of the town will manage to enjoy their game even when burdened with domestic cares, for one may often see a small boy or girl, seated on the edge of the pavement, nursing a baby on one arm and conducting a skilful game of knucklebones with the other.

CHAPTER XVIII

CHRISTMAS IN ROME

CHRISTMAS in Rome, as in all Christian countries, is especially the children's festival. As the December days grow shorter the shop-windows from an early hour in the afternoon are brilliantly lighted, and especially those where cakes, sweets, toys, and other pretty trifles are displayed, present a very festive appearance. The narrow pavements are crowded with family parties; small faces are pressed against the glass, and shrill childish voices may be heard

78

eagerly explaining to patient fathers and mothers what particular gifts are specially desired for the Twelfth-Night stocking.

For the Roman children do not receive their presents on Christmas Day, nor do they look to kindly, merry Santa Claus as the distributor of good things ; on the contrary, it is a lady known as the *Befana* who, on the Eve of the Epiphany, brings to each child the gifts she thinks he deserves. The *Befana*, though, of course, none of the children have actually seen her, is supposed to be rather forbidding in appearance, being tall, dark, imposing, and decidedly ugly. She enters the house during the night by way of the chimney, armed with a long cane, and carrying a bell, which she rings to announce her arrival. Though the darkness renders her invisible, the ringing of her bell and the rap of her stick on the floor are distinctly audible, and are heard with joyful expectation or trembling fear, according to the good or bad conscience of the listener. For the *Befana* has a stern sense of justice, and, though she brings beautiful and appropriate gifts to good, industrious children, naughty and idle ones may find that she has left nothing in their stockings but bags of ashes, which must, indeed, seem very like Dead Sea fruit, when one has been expecting rosy apples, golden oranges, packets of sweets, and *marrons glacés*, besides more enduring treasures.

Rome

But though Christmas itself is not the season for present-giving, it is celebrated in the churches with great pomp, and to many of the poorer children in Rome the sight of the beautiful *Presepio*, which is shown in the churches, is one of the greatest delights of the year.

The word *presepio* means simply a stable or manger, but in its special use denotes something far more elaborate and splendid.

It is at the ancient church of the Ara Cœli, near the Capitol, that the grandest *Presepio* is to be seen, for this church possesses a most precious statue of the *Bambino*, as the Christ-child is called in Italian. This *Bambino* is the object of great veneration, and is reported to have performed many miracles, curing the sick, and even bringing back to life those who were apparently at the point of death. Some of these wonderful cures may perhaps be accounted for by the fact that as soon as the aid of the *Bambino* was called in, the doctors ceased to attend the sufferer, and so gave him a better chance of life, for the constant bleeding and other drastic remedies in favour with Italian doctors of earlier times frequently exhausted the patient more than the illness itself, and the cessation of these allowed Nature to do her healing work undisturbed, with the result that the invalid regained his strength in what may have seemed a miraculous way.

IN THE CATACOMBS. *Chapter xv.*

Christmas in Rome

There is no doubt, however, that among the more ignorant people of Rome a firm belief in the miraculous powers of this statue of the *Bambino* still exists.

There is a popular legend that the statue was carved about five centuries ago by a Franciscan monk in Jerusalem out of olive-wood from Gethsemane. When the carving was finished the poor monk wished that he possessed the skill to paint the figure, and thus render it more lifelike, but, unable to do so and wearied with his toil, he fell asleep. In his dreams he thought he saw St. Luke himself painting the statue, and was filled with joy that his work should be so honoured ; and lo ! when he awoke, there stood the little image painted and finished as we see it now, though the monk had slept only a few moments. He set out for Rome without delay, and placed the statue in the Ara Cœli, where it may be seen to this day, splendidly dressed, and covered from head to foot with valuable jewels, which have been laid on its shrine as marks of gratitude for favours supposed to have been received from it.

On Christmas Day the *Presepio* is exhibited in one of the side chapels, which is transformed into a beautiful grotto. In front are life-size figures of Mary and Joseph, the former superbly dressed, and even adorned with diamond ear-rings. Just behind them stand the ox and the ass. At one side kneel the

Kings and shepherds in humble adoration, while above are represented cherubs and angels hovering over the group below.

In the background is painted a pastoral landscape ; shepherds are seen lying under the palm-trees keeping their sheep, which are covered with real snow-white wool. Besides these, there are figures of women carrying baskets of ripe fruit on their heads, and innumerable candles shed a soft brilliant light over the whole scene.

But it is not till about noon that the crowning feature is added to the group of figures when, during the High Mass, the jewelled *Bambino* is carried in solemn procession from the high altar to the *Presepio*, and placed on the knees of the Madonna, there to remain until Epiphany, when the image is taken back to its own shrine, and the spectacle of the *Presepio* is ended.

Meanwhile, every day from Christmas to Twelfth Night, a curious and interesting performance takes place in the Ara Cœli. At the west end of the church a high platform is erected, and here the children of the parish, most of them belonging to the poorer classes, come daily to recite the story of the wonderful Bambino to all who choose to listen. Usually one child recites alone, but sometimes a spirited dialogue is given, in which two or three take part. They have been well drilled and taught at school, but they go through their little performance without the aid, or even the presence, of their teachers; for whatever defects a Roman child may possess, shyness is certainly not one of them, and, quite unabashed by their audience, they preach their little sermon or recite their poem with complete self-possession, and with free and graceful gestures, which seem to come to them naturally and instinctively. Occasionally one of the very little children will forget and falter over her words, but she is speedily re-assured and assisted by an elder girl or boy, and will begin all over again quite confidently and happily. Altogether the children's performance at the Ara Cœli is one of the most interesting features of Christmas in Rome.

CHAPTER XIX

THE EASTER FESTIVAL

THE special ceremonies in connection with Easter may be said to begin on Palm Sunday, and during the week between that day and the great festival the churches are crowded with worshippers or sight-seers. The former usually attend their own parish churches, while the latter flock eagerly to St. Peter's or to the beautiful church of St. John Lateran, which is not only very large but enjoys the dis-tinction of being the oldest church in Rome.

Rome

On Palm Sunday, in the morning, the ceremony of blessing the palms takes place, and at St. Peter's this is accompanied by such fine music, and so much pomp and splendour, that the church is always crowded (chiefly with foreigners), and every seat is occupied from a very early hour. Those who cannot get seats walk about in the nave, which looks like a moving mass of people of all ages, from the very old, who, one might suppose, would be timid about mingling with such a crowd of pushing, excited people, to tiny babies in arms, sucking their thumbs and staring placidly about them, quite unmoved by the unusual stir. Every European nation seems to be represented in this motley assembly, and a subdued babel of various languages is heard until the actual ceremony begins, when a hush falls on all those who are near the altar, and comparative silence reigns throughout the great church.

After the great branches of palm and olive have been solemnly blessed they are distributed amongst the congregation, those who are seated in the front row receiving them from a priest, and breaking off twigs, which they hand to those behind them, until everyone who wishes has received some memento of Palm Sunday at St. Peter's.

This part of the service being completed, a procession is formed of all the clergy of many different degrees who have taken part in the ceremony ; the least important come first, and the stately and gorgeously robed figure of a Cardinal brings up the rear. The Romans love a crowd, but have very little idea of organizing its movements, so that as the throng press eagerly forward in their anxiety to see all that is to be seen, it is with difficulty that the officials who precede the procession are able to clear just sufficient space for it to pass. The great brazen doors at the west end of the church, which are only used on special occasions, stand wide open, and the procession passes through them on to the steps outside, where the hymn beginning " Glory and praise and honour be to Thee " is solemnly sung. The concourse of priests in their splendid vestments, standing in the bright sunlight, with the great pile of St. Peter's behind them, and the wide piazza below crowded with spectators, make an impressive spectacle ; the solemn music adds to the effect, and the whole scene is one which will not be soon forgotten by anyone who has witnessed it.

A pretty and interesting sight may often be seen at the entrance to the Vatican Palace on Palm Sunday, when companies of little girls, who have just made their First Communion, are granted an audience with the Pope, who solemnly blesses them on their entrance into a more responsible period of their lives. They are usually from about ten to thirteen years of age, and are dressed entirely in

Rome

white, from the veil and flowers which they wear on their heads, to the white kid shoes which complete their costume.

Shortly before Easter it is the custom for priests to visit the houses of their parishioners for the purpose of blessing their homes, and as it is impossible to visit every house on the same day, for a few days before the festival it is very usual to meet in the street a priest making his rounds, preceded by an acolyte carrying the holy water which is used in the ceremony.

Easter Eve is, however, the chief day for this visitation, and in many houses the food which is to be eaten on the following day is arranged on a large table in order that it may also be blessed by the priest. Such a table is often a very pretty sight, and suggests most agreeable prospects for the morrow. It is covered with a spotless white cloth, on which are set forth great dishes of eggs, fruit, butter, etc., and, to crown all, a large Easter cake beautifully iced and decorated.

During the week between Palm Sunday and Easter Day the already large number of strangers in Rome is increased by visitors from all parts of the world, who flock to the Eternal City to take part in the greatest festival of the year. Many of them are Catholic pilgrims, for whom Rome possesses a strong attraction, as being the residence of the Pope and the headquarters of their Church; but the greater

86

number are ordinary sightseers, curious to see all that is interesting, new, or beautiful, and looking upon the grand services and gorgeous ceremonies to be seen at St. Peter's much as they would regard any other spectacular entertainment. The whole city assumes an appearance of festivity, and, though during the Holy Week the church services are solemn and mournful in character, the streets and shops are at their gayest in preparation for the coming festival, hotels are crowded to overflowing, and carriages full of cheerful tourists roll along the streets. Even the cab-drivers look more than usually happy, for it is their harvest-time, fares being higher than at ordinary times, and tips larger and more plentiful.

On Easter Eve the bells of all the principal churches are rung, to usher in the coming joy of the Festival of the Resurrection, so that the cheerful sounds are heard in every quarter of the city; and almost with the dawn on Easter morning the churches throw open their doors and begin their services. High Mass at St. Peter's is a most splendid function, and the Cathedral Church, as the hour for the great service of the day approaches, presents much the same appearance as it did on Palm Sunday, except that the numbers present are much increased, and that it is still more difficult to get anywhere near the high altar, or to see anything of what is passing, though all may enjoy the beautiful music.

Rome

CHAPTER XX

BLESSING THE ANIMALS

EVERY year on January 21, which is the Festival of St. Agnes, a very quaint and interesting ceremony takes place in the old church, outside the walls, dedicated to the beautiful child-martyr. The name Agnes signifies *a lamb*, and the saint is often represented in pictures with a lamb, as the Christian symbol of gentleness and innocence, by her side. It is therefore very appropriate that this Church of St. Agnes should be the spot chosen for the annual ceremony known as the Blessing of the Lambs. On this occasion the church is always crowded to overflowing, so that it is difficult for those at a distance to see much of what is being done at the altar. The children, of whom there are generally a great number present, are allowed to stand on the seats, or are lifted up by their elders, in order that they may see over the heads of the crowd, and enjoy the spectacle of the procession to the altar, and the benediction of the two pretty little animals, who seem quite unconscious of the great honour for which they have been singled out.

The two lambs who form the central feature of this solemn function have been set apart and specially

THE BLESSING OF THE LAMBS ON THE
FESTIVAL OF ST AGNES. *Page 88*

tended from their birth, in order that their fleece when fully grown may be worthy of being woven into vestments for the Pope and Archbishops. They are chosen with the greatest care, and must be quite free from any kind of blemish. From the first their fleece receives the most scrupulous attention, being kept beautifully clean and regularly brushed. On the morning of the important ceremony, after being carefully washed and combed until their wool is snow-white and shining like floss-silk, the two lambs are brought to the church, and each one is placed in a satin-lined basket or cradle adorned with knots of ribbon and garlands of flowers. Two members of the Papal household in full uniform receive the baskets with their living freight, and with slow stately tread advance to the east end of the church, where they present the lambs before the altar to receive the blessing of the officiating priest, who on this occasion is usually a Cardinal or some other great personage.

As it is carefully arranged that the baby-lambs shall be in a rather sleepy state at the hour appointed for the benediction, the little creatures lie wonderfully still and passive, though a faint sound of bleating may occasionally be heard above the murmuring voice of the priest.

Meanwhile the ground outside the church presents a gay and lively scene, being covered with a motley crowd, composed of sightseers who have arrived too late to find places inside the building, idlers of all ages from the neighbourhood, and men, women, and children, bent on turning the occasion to profitable account, and who are driving a brisk trade, especially amongst the *forestieri*, or foreigners, whom they regard as their natural prey, by the sale of trifling souvenirs of the day—such as little white wax lambs in tiny cradles, and small pictures of St. Agnes with a lamb by her side.

The wax lambs, it is true, leave a good deal to the imagination of the buyer, for they look just as much like little pigs or kittens as like lambs; but as they may be bought complete in an ornamental cradle for the modest sum of a penny each, one must not be too critical. When the ceremony within comes to an end, those who are outside make a rush, eager to see what they can of the little pageant, which, however, is not much, as the lambs are quickly installed in the carriage awaiting them, and driven off in charge of their imposing guardians to the Vatican Palace, where the great Pontiff himself gives them his blessing. From the Vatican they are taken to the Convent of St. Cecilia in Trastevere, to remain there in charge of the nuns until Easter, when their wool is ready for shearing and weaving.

Another interesting custom which prevails in Rome is the annual blessing of the horses and other

Blessing the Animals

beasts of burden, which takes place at the Church of St. Antony on January 17. On the morning of this day the doors of the church are thrown wide open, and at the appointed hour a priest stations himself at the top of the steps, and prepares to bestow the blessing of the Church on the patient dumb creatures who spend their lives in the service of man, and on whom so much of the pleasure and the business of the great city depends. The animals pass in procession in front of the church steps, and the priest, dipping a great brush into holy water, sprinkles them generously, at the same time pronouncing a blessing on their labours for the year to come.

In the procession are to be found horses, mules, and donkeys of all sorts and sizes, for it includes not only fine carriage and riding horses belonging to wealthy citizens or great dignitaries of the Church, but the thin, spirited little cab-horses which ply their trade so willingly for long weary hours in the crowded streets, and even the sorriest little mules and donkeys, employed as beasts of burden by the humble street-hawker or costermonger.

The saint on whose festival this custom is observed is regarded as the special patron of dumb animals, being popularly known as *Sant' Antonio del Porco*, or St. Antony of the Pig, and his portrait may sometimes be seen hanging on the wall of a stable or cowshed, where it is to be hoped this reminder that the

merciful man is merciful to his beast may tend to
ameliorate the lot of the creatures that kindly
St. Antony loved to protect.

CHAPTER XXI

THE HORSEMAN ON THE JANICULUM

Though Rome is a very old city, Italy is a very young
kingdom, for it was only in 1861 that the numerous
small principalities, duchies, and republics into which
she was divided were finally united into one nation
under the rule of a King and Parliament.

We speak of Rome as a city, but her past history
is that of an Empire, for, owing to her widespread
conquests under the Emperors, and in later times
to the enormous power of the Papacy, she could claim
for many ages a foremost place among the nations
of Europe.

Julius Cæsar, as we all know, led his conquering
legions into every part of the known world, even to
the little savage island of Britain, which Virgil called
the farthest corner of the earth. It is true that
in time Imperial Rome was destined to decay, and
in her turn to be ravaged by invading forces; but
though she was overrun by savage tribes from
Germany, who so ruthlessly defaced her splendid
monuments and buildings that the word " Goth "

The Horseman on the Janiculum

or "Vandal" has come to signify one who has no respect for what is sacred or beautiful, Immortal Rome rose again from her ashes, and, owing to the enormous power wielded by the Papacy, became once more an important factor in the politics of Europe. For the Pope was a greater monarch than any mere earthly King or Emperor, possessing as he did spiritual as well as temporal power, and, accordnig to the common belief of Christendom, bearing in his hands the very keys of Heaven.

But by dint of striving for too much temporal power, the Popes gradually but surely undermined their own position, until after a long struggle they were finally deprived of all dominion outside the affairs of the Roman Church. Before this had been accomplished Rome had become as a house divided against itself, and was the home of great corruption and many dissensions. The rest of Italy, torn and weakened by constant quarrels among the different states, was overrun by the Austrians, and subject to them.

Then the great Napoleon arose, and, marching his troops into Italy, gained some brilliant victories over the Austrians. At first the Italians looked upon him as a deliverer, but they soon found they had merely exchanged one master for another.

Rome was occupied by French troops, and was converted into a French province, and when the

Rome

unhappy little son of Napoleon was born, his father
conferred on him the title of King of Rome. The
fall of Napoleon brought no relief to Italy, for Rome
still remained under French rule, and was garrisoned
by French soldiers, while the rest of the country
chafed under the hated exactions of Austria and
France. But when all seemed dark and almost
hopeless, the patriot-hero, who was destined to
rouse his country to throw off the dominion of the
foreigner and the Papacy, appeared in the person of
Giuseppe Garibaldi. The history of Garibaldi's life
is too long to be told here, and we will only say that
it is more romantic, thrilling, and inspiring than any
story of adventure and heroism to be found in fiction.
He was born in a humble position, but even from
his earliest childhood was remarkable for his great
natural courage, and for his generous and noble
character. Before he was eight he had rescued a
poor woman from drowning at the risk of his own
life, and at the age of twelve, by his promptitude
and daring, he saved the lives of a boat-load of his
companions. He was a handsome, manly-looking
boy, with beautiful frank blue eyes, and one of his
chief characteristics was his hatred of cruelty and
oppression in any form; above all he could not
endure to see a little child or a dumb animal ill-
treated.

As he grew older, and began to realize fully the

unhappy state of his country, his heart burned with indignation at the thought of her bitter wrongs, and the resolution to devote himself to her service grew up within him, and became the guiding principle of his life, though it was not until he had gained experience as a soldier, and had distinguished himself by his intrepidity and daring in South America, where he had gone as quite a young man, that he could begin to put the principle into practice.

Garibaldi was not a Roman, but Rome had a specially strong hold on his affections ; he had paid a visit to the city when quite a lad, and the sight of her dimmed glory made an impression on his mind and an appeal to his heart that lasted as long as he lived.

When in later years, in the prime of his strong manhood, he raised the standard of revolt in Italy, the powers arrayed against him seemed so over-whelming that only the strength of his enthusiasm and the magnetism of his great faith and courage enabled him to gather round him a little army of patriots, and to inspire them with something of his own brave and confident spirit.

When Garibaldi, with his little band, after much skirmishing and many hindrances, at last entered Rome, a terrible struggle ensued. The narrow streets near the Vatican ran with blood, and were heaped with dead or dying men. The patriots

Rome

fought desperately, showing the indomitable courage
of men who know their cause to be a righteous one,
but Rome and the French soldiers were too strong
for them, and finally they were forced to retreat,
and to take refuge in the mountain fastnesses.
Some eventually escaped by sea, others were captured
by the French or Austrians, and some, alas! were
betrayed into the hands of the enemy by their own
countrymen, for the sake of the price that was on
their heads. Garibaldi himself escaped at last, and,
regardless of the almost insuperable difficulties which
lay before him, set himself once more to the great
work of his life, with a courage and determination
which eventually brought success.

Rome, where he had suffered defeat and rejection,
became the capital of the New Italy which Garibaldi
and his patriots had built up, and a fine equestrian
statue of the national hero has been placed by the
Romans on the Janiculum, as a witness of his
patriotism and the nation's gratitude.

And so, looking down from the highest of her
seven hills, over the city he loved so well, the horse-
man on the Janiculum may be seen from many a
distant point, standing out against the sky, a symbol
of what a great faith, combined with a great courage,
can accomplish.

BILLING AND SONS, LTD., PRINTERS, GUILDFORD

PRICE **1/6** EACH

BLACK'S "PICTURES OF MANY LANDS" SERIES
AND OTHER SIMILAR BOOKS

Crown 4to., with picture in colour on the cover, each containing 58 illustrations, of which 32 are in colour.

The Children's World	How other People Live
The World in Pictures	Beasts and Birds
The British Isles in Pictures	Gardens in their Seasons
The British Empire in Pictures	Pictures of British History
Europe in Pictures	

NOTE.—These volumes are also to be had in cloth at 2s. *each.*

Large crown 8vo., cloth, with frontispiece.

Eric ; or, Little by Little	Julian Home : a Tale of College
St. Winifred's ; or, The World of	Life
School	

Scott's Waverley Novels. *See list at the end of this Catalogue.*

PRICE **1/6** NET EACH

RED CAP TALES FROM SCOTT

Large crown 8vo., cloth, each containing 8 full-page illustrations in colour.

Waverley	The Antiquary
Guy Mannering	Ivanhoe
Rob Roy	Fortunes of Nigel
The Pirate, and A Legend of	Quentin Durward
Montrose	

How to Use the Microscope. A Guide for the Novice. Containing 20 full-page illustrations from photo-micrographs, etc.	Gardening Birthday Book The Fairy Tales Birthday Book (*Autumn*, 1913) 12 full-page illustrations in colour in each

PUBLISHED BY A. AND C. BLACK, 4, 5 AND 6 SOHO SQUARE, LONDON, W.

Large crown 8vo., cloth, with picture in colour on the cover.

PEEPS AT MANY LANDS AND CITIES

Each containing 12 full-page illustrations in colour.

Australia	Denmark	*India	Panama
Belgium	Edinburgh	Ireland	Paris
Berlin	*Egypt	Italy	Portugal
British North	Egypt, Ancient	. Jamaica	Rome
Borneo	England	*Japan	*Russia
(*Autumn,* 1913)	Finland	Java	*Scotland
Burma	Florence	Kashmir	*Siam
Canada	France	Korea	South Africa
Ceylon	Germany	London	South Seas
*China	Greece	*Morocco	*Spain
Corsica	Holland	Newfoundland	Sweden
Cuba	Holy Land	New York	Switzerland
(*Autumn,* 1913)	Hungary	New Zealand	Turkey
Delhi and the	Iceland	Norway	Wales
Durbar			

* Also to be had in French at 2s. *net each. See " Les Beaux Voyages " Series.*
For Larger Series of " Peeps at Many Lands and Cities," see list of 3s. 6d. *net Books.*

PEEPS AT NATURE

Each containing 16 full-page illustrations, 8 of them in colour.

Bird Life of the Seasons	The Naturalist at the Sea-Shore
British Butterflies [Horsetails	Pond Life
British Ferns, Club-Mosses, and	Reptiles and Amphibians
British Land Mammals	Romance of the Rocks
British Moths	Wild Flowers and their Wonder-
Natural History of the Garden	ful Ways

PEEPS AT HISTORY

Each containing 8 full-page illustrations in colour, and 20 line drawings in the text.

America	Canada	India	Scotland
The Barbary Rovers	Holland	Japan	

PEEPS AT GREAT RAILWAYS

Canadian Pacific Railway	North-Eastern and Great Nor-
(*Autumn,* 1913)	thern Railways (in 1 volume)
Great Western Railway	South-Eastern and Chatham and
London and North-Western Rail-	London, Brighton and South
way	Coast Railways (in 1 volume)

PEEPS AT INDUSTRIES

Each containing 24 full-page illustrations from photographs.

Rubber	Sugar	Tea

OTHER "PEEPS" VOLUMES

Peeps at the Heavens	Peeps at the Life and Legends of
Peeps at Architecture (*Autumn,* 1913)	Other Lands (Norse and Lapp)
Peeps at Heraldry	(*Autumn,* 1913)
Peeps at the Navy (*Autumn,* 1913)	Peeps at the Life of Sir Walter
Peeps at Palaces (*Autumn,* 1913)	Scott (*Autumn,* 1913)

"HOMES OF MANY LANDS" SERIES

India.   Containing 12 full-page illustrations in colour.

PUBLISHED BY A. AND C. BLACK, 4, 5 AND 6 SOHO SQUARE, LONDON, W.

BEAUTIFUL BRITAIN

Large square demy 8vo., bound in cloth, each containing 12 full-page illustrations in colour.

Abbotsford
Cambridge
Canterbury
Channel Islands
English Lakes
Firth of Clyde
Isle of Arran

Isle of Man
Isle of Wight
Killarney
London
Oxford
Stratford-on-Avon
Leamington & Warwick

Peak Country
Thames
Trossachs
North Wales
Wessex
Westminster Abbey
Windsor and Eton

PRICE **2/=** NET EACH

LES BEAUX VOYAGES

(A SERIES OF "PEEPS AT MANY LANDS" IN FRENCH)

Large crown 8vo., cloth, each containing 12 full-page illustrations in colour and a sketch-map.

Algerie
Alsace
Chine
Ecosse

Egypte
Espagne
Indes
Indo·Chine

Japon
Maroc
Russie
Tunisie

PRICE **2/=** EACH

SCOTT'S WAVERLEY NOVELS.   *See list at the end of this Catalogue.*

PRICE **2/6** NET EACH

Containing 16 full-page illustrations from photographs.
What the Other Children do

BIBLIOTHÈQUE ROUGE EN COULEURS

BEAUTIFUL BOOKS IN FRENCH FOR YOUNG PEOPLE

Large crown 8vo., cloth, each containing 12 full-page illustrations in colour.

Les Contes de ma Grand'mère | Éric

PUBLISHED BY A. AND C. BLACK, 4, 5 AND 6 SOHO SQUARE, LONDON, W.

PRICE **2/6** EACH

Large crown 8vo., illustrated.

Stories of Old. *(Small crown 4to.)*
Eric ; or, Little by Little
St. Winifred's ; or, The World of School

Julian Home : A Tale of College Life
Scott's Waverley Novels. *See list at the end of this Catalogue.*

PRICE **3/6** NET EACH

PEEPS AT MANY LANDS AND CITIES

Larger Volumes in the style of the Popular One Shilling and Sixpenny net "PEEPS AT MANY LANDS AND CITIES" Series.

Each containing 32 full-page illustrations in colour.

The World
The British Empire
The Gorgeous East (India, Burma, Ceylon, and Siam)
The Far East (China, Japan, and Korea)
Oceania (Australia, New Zealand, and South Seas)

Large crown 8vo., cloth.

The Open Book of Nature : A Book of Nature Study for Young People. 16 full-page illustrations in colour and 114 reproductions from photographs, etc.

The Alps. 24 full-page illustrations from photographs

The Holy Land. *(Not illustrated)*

CONTES ET NOUVELLES

BEAUTIFUL BOOKS IN FRENCH FOR YOUNG PEOPLE.

Large square crown 8vo., cloth, each containing 12 full-page illustrations in colour.

Les Petits Aventuriers en Amérique
La Guerre aux Fauves
Un Tour en Mélanesie

La Case de l'Oncle Tom (8 pictures in colour and 16 in black and white)
Voyages de Gulliver

PUBLISHED BY A. AND C. BLACK, 4, 5 AND 6 SOHO SQUARE, LONDON, W.

GREAT BUILDINGS AND HOW TO ENJOY THEM

A SERIES OF HANDBOOKS FOR THE AMATEUR LOVER OF ARCHITECTURE

Square demy 8vo., cloth, each containing 48 full-page illustrations from photographs.

Early Christian and Byzantine Architecture	Greek Architecture
	Norman Architecture
Gothic Architecture	Romanesque Architecture

PRICE **3/6** EACH

LIFE STORIES OF ANIMALS

Large crown 8vo., cloth, each containing 8 full-page illustrations in colour.

The Black Bear	The Fowl	The Rat
The Cat	The Fox (*Autumn*, 1913)	The Squirrel
The Dog	The Lion	The Tiger

Large crown 8vo., cloth, illustrated.

In the Grip of the Wild Wa (*Autumn*, 1913)	By a Schoolboy's Hand
Tales of St. Austin's	Exiled from School
The Head of Kay's	From Fag to Monitor
Mike : A Public School Story	The Sea Monarch
The Gold Bat	The Scouts of Seal Island (*Autumn*, 1913)
Psmith in the City	Cook's Voyages and Discoveries
The Pothunters	Dana's Two Years Before the Mast
A Prefect's Uncle	The Divers
The White Feather	Stories from Waverley
The First Voyages of Glorious Memory (*Hakluyt*)	The Life of St. Paul
Nipping Bear	The Right Sort
The Adventures of Don Quixote	God's Lantern-Bearers
Park's Travels in the Interior of Africa	The Kinsfolk and Friends of Jesus
	The Story of Stories : A Life of Christ for the Young

PUBLISHED BY A. AND C. BLACK, 4, 5 AND 6 SOHO SQUARE, LONDON, W.

PRICE **3/6** EACH (*Continued*)

Large crown 8vo., cloth, illustrated.

Tales from Scottish Ballads
The Story of a Scout
Two Boys in War-Time
The Story of Robin Hood and His
    Merry Men
The Wolf Patrol
Jack Haydon's Quest
Red Men of the Dusk
The Saints in Story
The Vicar of Wakefield
The Mystery of Markham
                (*Autumn*, 1913)
Black Evans
J. O. Jones, and How He Earned
    His Living
Jim Mortimer
Green at Greyhouse
Tales of Greyhouse
Robinson Crusoe
Eric
St. Winifred's
Julian Home

Beasts of Business
Hero and Heroine
Stories. (*Ascott R. Hope*)
Half-Text History. (*No illustrations*)
Black and Blue
Cap and Gown Comedy
               (*No illustrations*)
All Astray
The King Who Never Died
The Bull of the Kraal
A Tale of the Time of the Cave
    Men
Tangerine : **A Child's Letters**
    from Morocco
Willy Wind, and Jock and the
    Cheeses
The Adventures of Oliver Twist
              (*Autumn*, 1913)
Life of Sir Walter Scott
Scott's Poetical Works
Scott's Waverley Novels. *See list
    at the end of this Catalogue*

PRICE **5/=** NET EACH

Large crown 8vo., cloth.
Through the Telescope
The Life and Love of the Insect
The Ramparts of Empire

Demy 4to. (oblong), cloth gilt.
Our Old Nursery Rhymes
Little Songs of Long Ago (*More
    Old Nursery Rhymes*)

PRICE **5/=** EACH

Crown 8vo., cloth.

Here and There. (*Illustrated*)
The Schoolboy Abroad

Ready-Made Romance
Dramas in Duodecimo

PUBLISHED BY A. AND C. BLACK, 4, 5 AND 6 SOHO SQUARE, LONDON, W.

(6)

PRICE **6/=** EACH

Small square demy 8vo., cloth, with illustrations in colour.

Grimm's Fairy Tales
Æsop's Fables
The Arabian Nights (*Autumn*, 1913)
Hans Andersen's Fairy Tales
Swiss Family Robinson
The Fairchild Family (*Autumn*, 1913)
The Pilgrim's Progress
Uncle Tom's Cabin
Adventurers in America
The Children's Book of Stars
The Children's Book of Edinburgh
The Children's Book of Gardening
The Children's Book of Art
The Children's Book of London

The Children's Book of Celtic Stories
Children's Tales of English Minsters
Russian Wonder Tales
Tales from "The Earthly Paradise" (*Autumn*, 1913)
Gulliver's Travels into Several Remote Nations of the World
Talks about Birds
Red Cap Tales
Red Cap Adventures
The Tales of a Grandfather
The Book of the Railway

A LIST OF CHEAPER BOOKS SUITABLE FOR YOUNG PEOPLE
PUBLISHED AT 1s. 0d., 9d., and 6d. EACH

PRICE **1/=** EACH

Eric; or, Little by Little
St. Winifred's; or, The World of School

Julian Home; a Tale of College Life

PRICE **1/=** NET EACH

TALES OF ENGLISH MINSTERS

Large crown 8vo., each containing 6 full-page illustrations.

| Canterbury | Ely | Lincoln | St. Paul's |
| Durham | Hereford | St. Albans | York |

Scott's Waverley Novels. Crown 8vo., cloth, each volume containing a frontispiece in colour. *See list at the end of this Catalogue*

PRICE **9d.**

Black's Painting Book for Children. By Agnes Nightingale. Containing 23 page outline pictures for colouring. Small crown 4to., bound in attractive cover

PUBLISHED BY A. AND C. BLACK, 4, 5 AND 6 SOHO SQUARE, LONDON, W.

PRICE **6d.** EACH

Demy 8vo., picture paper covers.

*Eric; or, Little by Little
*St. Winifred's ; or, The World of School

*Julian Home : a Tale of College Life

Scott's Waverley Novels. *See list following*

* *These may be had bound together in cloth cover for* **2s. 6d.**

THE WAVERLEY NOVELS
By SIR WALTER SCOTT

The Authentic Editions of Scott are published solely by A. and C. BLACK, who purchased along with the copyright the interleaved set of the Waverley Novels in which Sir Walter Scott noted corrections and improvements almost to the day of his death. The under-noted editions have been collated word for word with this set, and many inaccuracies, some of them ludicrous, corrected.

LIST OF THE NOVELS

Waverley
Guy Mannering
The Antiquary
Rob Roy
Old Mortality
Montrose, and Black Dwarf
The Heart of Midlothian
The Bride of Lammermoor
Ivanhoe
The Monastery
The Abbot
Kenilworth
The Pirate

The Fortunes of Nigel
Peveril of the Peak
Quentin Durward
St. Ronan's Well
Redgauntlet
The Betrothed, etc.
The Talisman
Woodstock
The Fair Maid of Perth
Anne of Geierstein
Count Robert of Paris
The Surgeon's Daughter, etc.

For Details regarding Editions and Prices see below.

LIST OF EDITIONS OF THE WAVERLEY NOVELS

New Popular Edition. 25 Volumes. Price **6d.** per Volume.
The Portrait Edition. 25 Volumes. Price 1/- net per Volume.
Victoria Edition. 25 Volumes. Price 1/6 per Volume.
Two Shilling Edition. 25 Volumes. Price **2/-** per Volume.
Standard Edition. 25 Volumes. Price **2/6** per Volume.
Dryburgh Edition. 25 Volumes. Price **3/6** per Volume.

PUBLISHED BY A. AND C. BLACK, 4, 5 AND 6 SOHO SQUARE, LONDON, W.